SAT®

All-Nighter

SPARKNOTES

SparkNotes would like to thank Ben Paris for his contributions to this book and
Eric Goodman for his role as series editor.

© 2008 Spark Publishing

Interior icon © Matt Wiegle

SPARKNOTES is a registered trademark of SparkNotes LLC.

Spark Publishing
A Division of Barnes & Noble
120 Fifth Avenue
New York, NY 10011

Library of Congress Cataloging-in-Publication Data

SAT All-Nighter.
    p. cm.
  ISBN-13: 978-1-4114-0521-9 (pbk.)
  ISBN-10: 1-4114-0521-8 (pbk.)
  1. SAT (Educational Test)—Study Guides.

LB2353.57.S24 2008
378.1'662—dc22
                                    2008001476

Printed in the United States

Contents

Introduction

HAVE YOU EVER HAD A DREAM WHERE YOU'RE ABOUT TO take a crucial final exam and realize you haven't attended a single class all semester? Or that you're about to make a major presentation in front of hundreds of people only to realize you're standing there in your underwear? Well, we can't help you with that last one . . . but if that first dream is coming true—your SAT is fast approaching and you've barely begun to prepare— then you've come to the right place.

SparkNotes' *SAT All-Nighter* is intended to provide you with the largest leap in SAT proficiency in the shortest amount of time. If your test is a week away, or even if it's just one or two nights before the test and you need a last-minute crash course, this book provides a number of key strategies and techniques that will help you on test day.

Before we begin, we urge you to adopt a positive mindset for the task ahead. Why you're in your present predicament is of no concern. Maybe you've been busy at school, at work, or with family responsibilities. Maybe your dog ate your SAT homework. Who knows, and who cares? The point is that you still have some time before your test, and you need to make the most of it. You may feel that you're already behind the eight ball, but the point of this book is to show you that definite improvement is possible in the short term if you put in some effort each day to learn and absorb the information we present.

HOW TO USE THIS BOOK

Following this section, you'll encounter our SAT mini-test. This will give you a quick taste of the types of questions you can expect to encounter on the

SAT. More important, you can easily get a rough sense of your strengths and weaknesses and focus your study time accordingly.

The heart of this book consists of five "Intensives"—chapters that *intensely* distill the most important elements of the SAT. These Intensives cover the fundamentals—what you absolutely need to know for test day.

We've designed the Intensives so that you can work through each one in a few hours. Each Intensive has expert strategies, step methods, techniques, and practice questions to give you the opportunity to apply what you've learned. If you have time to work through the whole book, by all means do so. But if you don't, use the mini-test to help you decide which parts of the book might be most valuable *for you* at this stage of the game. We conclude with the Top 15 Test-Day Tips, designed to help you put your best test-taking foot forward on the big day.

SAT BASICS

The SAT is 3 hours and 45 minutes long. It has three major sections—Writing, Critical Reading, and Math—divided into ten smaller, timed sections. A perfect score is 2400. Read on for more info . . .

Structure

Of the ten sections you'll see on test day, nine are scored, and one is an unscored, experimental section. This unscored section will always be 25 minutes long, but it could be Writing, Critical Reading, or Math. You won't know which sections are scored and which one isn't, so treat every section as if it were scored.

Here's how the SAT breaks down:

SECTION	NUMBER OF QUESTIONS	TIME	SCORED
Writing (the Essay)	n/a	25 minutes	✓
Writing	35	25 minutes	✓
Critical Reading	24	25 minutes	✓
Critical Reading	24	25 minutes	✓
Critical Reading	19	20 minutes	✓
Math	20	25 minutes	✓
Math	18	25 minutes	✓
Math	16	20 minutes	✓
Experimental	18–35	25 minutes	✗
Writing	14	10 minutes	✓

The 25-minute Essay always comes first, and the 10-minute Writing section always comes last. The other eight sections, including the experimental section, may come in any order.

WRITING

SAT Writing tests your writing skills in two ways, across three timed sections. In all, the writing sections contain 49 multiple-choice questions:

- An Essay
- 25 Improving Sentences
- 18 Identifying Sentence Errors
- 6 Improving Paragraphs

These questions appear in one 25-minute section, which can come at any time during the SAT, and one 10-minute section, which comes last. We cover the Essay in Intensive 1 and the multiple-choice questions in Intensive 2.

CRITICAL READING

SAT Critical Reading is made up of three timed sections: Two of the timed sections are 25 minutes long each, and one is 20 minutes long. In all, the Critical Reading sections contain 67 questions:

- 19 Sentence Completions (SCs)
- 48 Reading Passages Questions

These two question types will be interspersed throughout the sections. We cover Sentence Completions in Intensive 3 and Reading Passages in Intensive 4.

MATH

SAT Math has two types of questions: multiple mhoice and student-produced response (which we'll call *grid-ins*). In all, the math sections contain 54 questions, across three timed sections:

- **25-minute section with 20 questions:** All questions are multiple choice
- **25-minute section with 18 questions:** 8 multiple choice and 10 grid-ins
- **20-minute section with 16 questions:** All questions are multiple choice

---

We cover math in Intensive 5.

Scoring

Your SAT score is based on what's known as your *raw score*. This score is affected by what you do to a particular question:

- **Get It Right:** You get 1 point.
- **Get It Wrong:** You lose a quarter point.
- **Leave It Blank:** You get 0 points.

Based on the raw scores of every test taker who took a particular SAT, the test makers work out a mathematical curve, then feed your raw score into a computer and get what's known as your *scaled score*. The scaled score takes your raw score on each section and converts it into a number between 200 and 800. Your official SAT score is the sum of the scaled scores on each of the three major sections, and 2400 is the perfect SAT score. The average score on each of the three sections is a little over 500, so the average score on the SAT is about 1520.

Registering for the Test

The fastest way to register for the SAT is to sign up at **www.collegeboard. com**. You can also register by mail, using an *SAT Registration Bulletin*, available at your school counselor's office. Either way, the SAT costs about $45.

When to Take the SAT

The SAT is offered seven times a year: January, March, May, June, October, November, and December. Most students take the SAT for the first time in the spring of their junior years—that means either in March or May. Depending on their scores, many students then decide to take the test again in the fall of their senior years. If you're planning to take the test a second time, make sure you take it early enough so that your scores will reach colleges before the application deadline passes. Bottom line: Check with the schools to which you are applying and make sure that you're on track to take the test by the correct date.

GENERAL SAT STRATEGIES

We'll spend the rest of this Introduction discussing some general SAT pointers to keep in mind before you immerse yourself in the mini-test and Intensives. These strategies apply to every section of the SAT. We list them here because you should always have these rules in the back of your mind as you study and, eventually, as you take the SAT:

- Set a Target Score
- Know the Instructions
- Use the Booklet As Scratch Paper
- Answer Easy Questions First
- Guess Intelligently
- Don't Be Afraid to Bail
- Avoid Carelessness
- Mine the Experience

You don't need to focus on them obsessively, but you should be sure not to forget these general strategies. They will help you save time and cut down on careless errors.

Set a Target Score

Before you begin studying for the SAT, you need to set a realistic scoring goal. This is a good strategy for any test taker but applies even more to those working within a short preparation time frame. To set a target score, take a look at the average SAT scores at the colleges to which you're applying. You should try to get a score that's a few points higher than the average at your first-choice school.

If you're gunning for a perfect score, you'll need to answer just about every question correctly. But if you're looking to score something a little less ambitious, you can probably skip or guess on questions that are really long or on question types that give you trouble.

Know the Instructions

You'll need all the time you can get, so don't waste time reading the test instructions during the actual test. Each Intensive begins with an X-ray in which we decode the directions for each section. Review them now so that you can skim them on test day. You should also go ahead and memorize the formulas in the Math Reference Area that precedes every SAT Math section.

Use the Booklet As Scratch Paper

You should write down all your work for math problems, in case you want to return to them later to complete the question or check your answer. But you should also make notes alongside the Critical Reading passages; doing so will help you stay on track when answering the subsequent questions. In addition, if you want to skip a question and come back to it later, you should make a distinctive mark next to it so that you won't miss it on your second pass through the questions.

Answer Easy Questions First

All questions are worth the same number of points, so there's no reason to slave away over a difficult question if doing so requires several minutes. In the same amount of time, you probably could have racked up points by answering a bunch of easy, less time-consuming questions. On the easy questions, you should be going faster so that you can save up time to figure out the harder problems. Since the SAT lets you skip around within a section, you should answer the easy and moderate questions first. If you come across a tough question, circle it and move on. That way you'll make sure that you get to see all the questions on the test that you have a good shot of getting right, while saving the leftover time for the difficult questions.

Remember, though, that which questions are easy or moderate and which are difficult is largely up to you. Generally speaking, SAT Math questions are ordered by level of difficulty, with easier questions coming first and harder questions coming later in the section. So are Sentence Completions. But in reality, it doesn't matter how the test makers have ordered the questions—whether by difficulty or by content tested. What matters is how easy or hard *you* find the questions. As you work through each test, trust your instincts: If you think a question is easy, it probably is. Figure out the answer and move on to the next one. If you think a question is hard, flag it and come back to it, once you've answered the easier questions.

Guess Intelligently

If you have five possible answer choices and you choose one randomly, you have a 20 percent chance of choosing the right one. If, however, you were able to narrow the choices down to four or even three, you'd significantly increase your odds of choosing the correct answer. The point is, you should guess intelligently—not randomly—on the SAT.

The SAT's wrong-answer penalty is strategically designed to eliminate any gain you might get from guessing randomly. But if you can eliminate even one answer choice, you should go ahead and guess from the remaining choices. That's guessing intelligently!

There's no wrong-answer penalty on the student-produced response math questions (what we call *grid-ins*). If you guess and get one wrong, you won't lose any points. If you've worked out a grid-in problem and have an answer, go ahead and grid it in. Even if you're unsure, filling in an answer can't hurt.

Don't Be Afraid to Bail

If you've spent a significant amount of time on a problem and haven't gotten close to answering it, let it go. Leaving a question unfinished may seem like giving up or wasting time you've already spent, but you can come back to the problem after you've answered the easy ones. The time you spent on the problem earlier won't be wasted. When you come back to the problem, you'll already have done part of the work needed to solve it.

Avoid Carelessness

It's easy to make mistakes if you're moving too quickly through the questions. Speeding through the test can result in misinterpreting a question or missing a crucial piece of information. You should always be aware of this kind of error because the test makers have written the test with speedy test takers in mind: Test makers often include tempting "partial answers" among the answer choices. A partial answer is the result of some, but not all, of the steps needed to solve a problem. If you rush through a question, you may mistake a partial answer for the real answer.

You should also be careful when bubbling in your answers. It goes without saying that you should pay attention to the letters being bubbled. You might try bubbling in groups (five at a time or a page at a time) rather than answering one by one. Circle the answers in the test booklet as you go through the page, and then transfer the answers over to the answer sheet as a group. This method should increase your speed and accuracy in filling out the answer sheet. To further increase your accuracy, say the question number and the answer in your head as you fill out the grid: "Number 1, **A**. Number 2, **C**. Number 3, **D**."

Mine the Experience

You'll want to review every practice question in order to reinforce what each one teaches for test day. "Well duh," you're probably thinking. "Of course, I'm going to see if I got it right, and check what I did wrong if I didn't." But you've got to go beyond that: Did you get it right for the right reason? Did you just get lucky, or is the process you used repeatable in the future? If you got it wrong, was your mistake simply careless, or does it indicate a lack of understanding regarding a particular concept? Each question offers a wealth of information, and the more you get out of each one, the fewer questions you'll need to do to bump up your score in the time remaining before the test. We therefore implore to you "mine the experience" of every exercise and example we present in this book.

On to the SAT mini-test!

SAT Mini-Test

THE FOLLOWING MINI-TEST INCLUDES EXAMPLES OF THE types of questions found in each of the scored sections of the SAT (minus the Essay). An answer key follows. If you have the time, work fully through all the Intensives. If you don't, use your performance on this mini-test to budget your time accordingly.

WRITING

> Directions for Identifying Sentence Errors: The sentences that follow assess whether you can recognize grammatical and usage errors. Every sentence is either grammatically correct or has one and only one error. If there is an error, the error will be lettered and underlined. Select the underlined part that must be fixed in order to make the sentence correct and error free. If the sentence is correct and error-free, choose E.

1. <u>Even though</u> Esther created a petition to protest the <u>crowning</u> of a prom queen,
   A   B
   <u>there is</u> many people who refused to sign, saying they support the <u>1950s-era</u>
   C   D
   tradition. <u>No error</u>
              E

2. <u>Neither</u> Kylie <u>nor</u> Jason <u>measure</u> up to <u>Carrie</u>. <u>No error</u>
   A   B   C   D   E

Directions for Improving Sentences: The sentences that follow assess whether you can identify and correct grammatical and usage errors, as well as recognize sentences that correctly adhere to the rules of standard written English.

A part of a sentence or the entire sentence will be underlined. Answers B–E consist of new ways of stating the underlined material; answer A is the same as the original sentence. Choose A if the original sentence is correct and produces the most effective sentence. Otherwise, choose one of the other answers.

In choosing answers, follow the requirements of standard written English and consider pay attention to grammar, choice of words, sentence construction, and punctuation. Your answer should create the best sentence—clear and precise, without awkwardness or ambiguity.

3. Eager to pass his final exams, <u>studying was the student's top priority</u>.

   (A) studying was the student's top priority.
   (B) the student made studying his top priority.
   (C) the top priority of the student was studying.
   (D) the student's top priority was studying.
   (E) studying was the top priority for the student.

4. Like the Byzantines, who in the course of ruling the eastern Mediterranean basin for a thousand years left behind much-imitated traditions in law, art, and architecture, <u>Ottoman architecture often features huge domes</u>.

   (A) Ottoman architecture often features huge domes.
   (B) Ottomans often features huge domes.
   (C) Ottomans often built huge domes.
   (D) huge domes were often featured by Ottoman architecture.
   (E) Ottoman architecture often featured huge domes.

Directions for Improving Paragraphs: The paragraphs that follow comprise an early essay draft. Some paragraphs or parts of the essay need revising and rewriting.

Some questions ask about specific aspects of sentences or of the essay, requiring you to revise structure or fix language. Other questions require you to redo organization or reorder the progression of ideas. When answering the questions, adhere to the rules of standard written English.

(1) Japanese cuisine continues to grow in popularity in the United States. (2) Americans are already fond of Chinese food. (3) Now they are discovering that Japanese cuisine takes a similar set of basic ingredients and transforms them into something quite special. (4) That Japanese food is generally low in fat and calories, and offers many options for vegetarians and vegans, adds to its popularity.

(5) Americans' enjoyment of Japanese cooking is still largely limited to an occasional night out at a Japanese restaurant. (6) Actually, Japanese cooking is surprisingly simple. (7) Anyone with a standard set of cooking utensils and knowledge of basic cooking terms can easily follow the recipes in any Japanese cookbook.

(8) Since Japanese restaurants tend to be fairly expensive, one would think that fans of the cuisine would be excited about the possibility of making it at home. (9) Unfortunately, many traditional Japanese recipes call for costly ingredients that often can only be found at Asian grocery stores. (10) As these ingredients become more widely available at lower prices, we are sure to see a proportional increase in the number of people cooking Japanese food at home.

5. In context, what is the best way to revise and combine sentences 2 and 3 (reproduced below)?

Americans are already fond of Chinese food. Now they are discovering that Japanese cuisine takes a similar set of basic ingredients and transforms them into something quite special.

(A) American people are already fond of Chinese food, and have discovered that Japanese cuisine takes a similar set of basic ingredients and transforms them into something quite special.

(B) American people are already fond of Chinese food, and now discover that Japanese cuisine takes a similar set of basic ingredients and transforms them into something quite special.

(C) Already fond of Chinese food, American people are now discovering that Japanese cuisine takes a similar set of basic ingredients and transforms them into something quite special.

(D) Already fond of Chinese food, having discovered that Japanese cuisine takes a similar set of basic ingredients and transforms them into something quite special, American people like it.

(E) American people are already fond of Chinese food; however, they are discovering that Japanese cuisine takes a similar set of basic ingredients and transforms them into something quite special.

6. In context, what is the best word to add to the beginning of sentence 5?

(A) Yet,

(B) Moreover,

(C) Predictably,

(D) Fortunately,

(E) Undoubtedly,

CRITICAL READING

Directions for Sentence Completions: Each of the following sentences has had a word or phrase removed and replaced with a blank. Select the word or phrase that, when put back into sentence, produces the best possible sentence.

1. In the Middle Ages, when few women held true political power, the irrepressible Eleanor of Aquitaine ------- England while her son, Richard the Lionhearted, tramped through Europe and the Middle East on the First Crusade.

   (A) domesticated   (B) ruled   (C) destroyed
       (D) betrayed   (E) repressed

2. The drummer's playing was so ------- that the other instruments couldn't be heard above the din.

   (A) quiet   (B) poor   (C) loud
       (D) enthusiastic   (E) fast

3. Ignoring criticisms that the film was excessively ------- and biased, the director resisted efforts to make changes designed to produce a less fierce, more ------- story.

   (A) placid . . prejudicial
   (B) tranquil . . neutral
   (C) brutal . . unfair
   (D) violent . . even-handed
   (E) long . . compact

Directions for Reading Passages: Use the introductory material and the passage
below to answer the questions that follow. Answer the questions based on the
content of the passage.

*The following passage is taken from an article on the architecture of the Etruscans,
a tribe that dominated Italy before the rise of the Romans, and the Roman architect
Vitruvius's* On Architecture, *which was written in the first century B.C. during the
reign of the emperor Augustus.*

Line   As we have seen, decades of archeological research have shown that
    Vitruvius's famous chapter on Etruscan temples idealized readily apparent
    diversity. Although Vitruvius did accurately capture the main features of the
    Etruscan style, actual Etruscan temples deviated quite significantly from his
5   ideal. We might ask why Vitruvius ignored the architectural diversity of the
    many different Etruscan temples with which he clearly was familiar. Answering
    this question provides some useful insight into not only Vitruvius's definition of the
    Etruscan style but also the purpose of *On Architecture* as a whole.
        Traditionally, scholars answered this question by pointing to Vitruvius's
10 allegiance to Greek philosophy. In chapter six, Vitruvius reports that he
    has had the benefit of a liberal Greek education, which he recommends to
    all aspiring architects. Without such broad training, Vitruvius argues, no
    architect can understand proper architectural theory. For Vitruvius,
    architectural theory rested on the principles of mathematical proportion
15 promulgated by such Greek philosophers as Pythagoras. These philosophers
    believed that the universe was structured according to god-given mathematical
    laws. They further believed that the harmonious mathematical structure of
    the universe (the *macrocosm*) was reflected in the structure of the human
    body (the *microcosm*). Vitruvius extended this reflection to architectural
20 forms. Temples, Vitruvius believed, must reflect the mathematical
    proportionality of the body, just as the body reflects the mathematical
    proportionality of the universe. Thus, Vitruvius claimed to "find"
    correspondences between proportional measurements of the human body—
    that the hand's length is one-tenth the body's height, for example—and
25 proportional measurements of the Etruscan temple. Vitruvius Hellenized
    the Etruscan temple by superimposing Greek notions of mathematical
    proportionality on his purportedly empirical description of the Etruscan
    temple style.
        Vitruvius's belief that specific natural proportions should be extended
30 to architectural forms does help to explain why he idealized Etruscan

temples. After all, mathematical models generally don't allow for much deviation. However, far more mundane considerations acted in concert with Vitruvius's allegiance to Greek notions of mathematical harmony to encourage the idealization of the Etruscan temple.

35   Despite its title, *On Architecture* was not written primarily for architects. It was written to convince the emperor Augustus, the most powerful patron in Rome, to give Vitruvius the opportunity to do large-scale architectural work. Vitruvius knew that if Augustus devoted any time at all to *On Architecture*, the emperor would most likely do what busy executives still
40   do to this day: He would read the introductions to each of the ten chapters and skip the rest of the book. Reading *On Architecture* in this manner— each introduction in sequence—is a revelation. One quickly realizes that the chapter introductions constitute an ancient résumé designed to convince Augustus to entrust part of his architectural legacy to Vitruvius.

45   Moreover, one must also keep in mind that *On Architecture*, like all ancient books, was originally published as a series of scrolls. Each modern "chapter" most likely corresponds to one ancient scroll. This physical form lent even greater significance to the snappy, pertinent introductions and the concise writing that modern readers also demand. The physical act of
50   reading a scroll made the kind of flipping back and forth that modern paginated books allow significantly more inconvenient. Scrolls strongly encouraged ancient authors to front-load the most important ideas they wanted to convey. The ancient author had to earn each "unrolling" by concentrating that much more on the order in which ideas were presented
55   and the economy with which they were expressed—and how much more so when one's intended audience is the emperor of Rome?

Vitruvius's idealization of Etruscan temples now becomes even more understandable. Tellingly, Vitruvius buried his discussion of Etruscan temples toward the end of a chapter (i.e., scroll), which reveals that
60   Vitruvius considered Etruscan temples to be relatively unimportant. In the unlikely event that Augustus (or his appointed reader) might have actually put in the effort to reach this discussion, the last thing Vitruvius would have wanted his exalted audience to encounter is any unnecessary detail. In order to capture Augustus' attention—and patronage—Vitruvius had to
65   demonstrate his complete command of architecture in the smallest, most easily digestible package possible. The purpose of *On Architecture* was not to record architectural variety in encyclopedic detail but rather to gain architectural commissions. This fact, along with Vitruvius's fundamental belief in proportionality, goes a long way toward explaining why Vitruvius
70   ignored the architectural diversity he doubtless saw in Etruscan temples.

4. As used in line 11, the word "liberal" most nearly means

(A) tolerant
(B) generous
(C) free-thinking
(D) wide-ranging
(E) narrow

5. On the whole, the author's attitude toward the traditional scholarly explanation of Vitruvius's description of the Etruscan temple style described in lines 12–32 is one of

(A) indifference
(B) respect
(C) frustration
(D) interest
(E) mistrust

6. The principal function of the fifth paragraph (lines 43–53) is to show

(A) that contemporary architects did not find *On Architecture* helpful to their work
(B) why Vitruvius ended up building so many structures for Augustus
(C) how Vitruvius constructed *On Architecture*'s ten chapters with his audience's likely reading habits in mind
(D) that Augustus was as busy as any modern-day executive
(E) how the nature of ancient scrolls discouraged readers

7. The author would most likely agree that the physical form of ancient books

    (A) prevented ancient authors from writing as well as modern authors

    (B) encouraged the writing of encyclopedic overviews

    (C) was responsible for the spread of ancient knowledge

    (D) is a unique source of insight into ancient writing largely ignored by traditional scholars

    (E) undermined the ability of ancient authors to gain patrons

8. The main purpose of the passage is to

    (A) expose Vitruvius's dishonesty

    (B) prove the value of a Greek education

    (C) suggest that Vitruvius considered Etruscan temples to be the most important type of temple

    (D) discuss the differences between ancient scrolls and modern books

    (E) account for the difference between Vitruvius's written description of Etruscan temples and their archaeological remains

MATH

Directions for Multiple Choice: Answer each question, using any available space for notes or figuring.

Notes:

1. The use of a calculator is permitted. All numbers used are real numbers.

2. Figures that accompany problems in this test are intended to provide information useful in solving the problems. They are drawn as accurately as possible EXCEPT when it is stated in a specific problem that the figure is not drawn to scale. All figures lie in a plane unless otherwise indicated.

3. Unless otherwise specified, the domain of any function f is assumed to be the set of all real numbers x for which $f(x)$ is a real number.

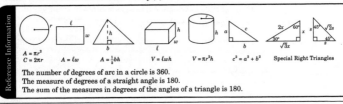

$A = \pi r^2$
$C = 2\pi r$

$A = \ell w$

$A = \frac{1}{2}bh$

$V = \ell wh$

$V = \pi r^2 h$

$c^2 = a^2 + b^2$

Special Right Triangles

The number of degrees of arc in a circle is 360.
The measure of degrees of a straight angle is 180.
The sum of the measures in degrees of the angles of a triangle is 180.

---

1. A classroom contains 31 chairs, some of which have arms and some of which do not. If the room contains 5 more armchairs than chairs without arms, how many armchairs does it contain?

(A) 10
(B) 13
(C) 16
(D) 18
(E) 21

2. What is the value of x if $3x - 27 = 33$?

(A) 2
(B) 11
(C) 20
(D) 27
(E) 35

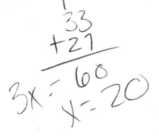

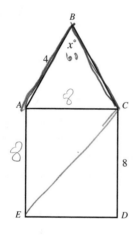

3. If $AB = BC$ and $x = 60$, what is the length of CE in rectangle $ACDE$?

(A)   4
(B) $4\sqrt{5}$
(C) $5\sqrt{2}$
(D)   8
(E)   12

Directions for Grid-Ins:

The following questions require you to solve the problem and enter your answer by marking the ovals in the special grid as shown in the examples below.

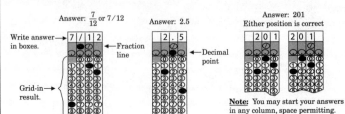

- Mark no more than one oval in any column.

- Because the answer sheet will be machine-scored, **you will receive credit only if the ovals are filled in completely.**

- Although not required, it is suggested that you write your answer in the boxes at the top of the columns to help you fill in the ovals accurately.

- Some problems may have more than one correct answer. In such cases, grid only one answer.

- No question has a negative answer.

- **Mixed numbers** such as $2\frac{1}{2}$ must be gridded as 2.5 or 5/2. If $2\;1\;/\;2$ is gridded, it will be interpreted as $\frac{21}{2}$, not $2\frac{1}{2}$.)

Note: You may start your answers in any column, space permitting. Columns not needed should be left blank.

- **Decimal Accuracy:** If you obtain a decimal answer, **enter the most accurate value the grid will accommodate.** For example, if you obtain an answer such as 0.6666 . . . , you should record the result as .666 or .667. **Less accurate values such as .66 or .67 are not acceptable.** Acceptable ways to grid $\frac{2}{3}$ = .666 . . .

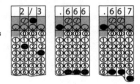

4. The original price of a banana in a store is $2. During a sale, the store reduces the price by 25%, and Joe buys the banana. Joe then raises the price of the banana 10% from the price at which he bought it and sells it to Sam. How much does Sam pay for the banana?

5. What is 0.5% of 55?

ANSWER KEY

WRITING

1. C   4. C
2. C   5. C
3. D   6. A

CRITICAL READING

1. B   5. B
2. C   6. C
3. D   7. D
4. D   8. E

MATH

1. D   4. 1.70
2. C   5. 0.275
3. B

PLAN YOUR ATTACK

Now that you've gotten a taste of the questions on each of the scored SAT sections, stop to think how you might best budget your time in the days and/ or week ahead. Full explanations to each of the mini-test questions are contained in the Intensives, but feel free to skip material on question types you feel you have under control. Or dive right in at the beginning and see how far you get—it's up to you.

Our set of SAT Intensives begins in the next chapter with the SAT Essay.

INTENSIVE 1

Writing Section:
The Essay

Essay X-ray

Essential Concepts

Essential Strategy

Practice Set

THE SAT ESSAY ALWAYS COMES FIRST, AND IT LASTS FOR 25 minutes. Basically, the test makers want to see how well you can write. This Intensive explains how to write a successful SAT essay in a short period of time.

ESSAY X-RAY

The SAT Essay has two main components: the directions and the topic. The directions don't change, so read them now so that you don't spend extra time with them on test day.

Directions: In this section, you are given 25 minutes to write an essay. You must write on the topic provided; an essay that is not on the topic provided will receive a 0.

Write your essay on the lines given on your answer sheet. People who are unfamiliar with your penmanship and style of writing will grade your essay, so print or write neatly and legibly.

As you write your essay, carefully consider grammar, tone, word choice, organization, logic, and other elements of style and argumentative writing. The essay is your chance to demonstrate your ability to successfully communicate and articulate ideas.

The directions are telling you to stick to the topic, develop your ideas, write legibly, and use the paper the SAT proctors give you. You probably would have done all that without the directions. On to the topic:

Think carefully about the issue presented in the following excerpt and the assignment below.

> "It is a mistake to suppose that men succeed through success; they much oftener succeed through failures. Precept, study, advice, and example could never have taught them so well as failure has done."
>
> —Samuel Smiles, Scottish author (1812–1904)

Assignment:

Is there truly no success like failure? Plan and write an essay in which you develop your point of view on this issue. Support your position with reasoning and examples taken from your reading, studies, experience, or observations.

On test day, you'll typically get some kind of quote, and then you'll get an "assignment" directing you to write about it. Pay careful attention here. Make sure you're clear on your assignment because off-topic essays get scores of zero. Our sample assignment asks you to develop your point of view on the issue presented in the Smiles quotation. Essentially, the test makers want you to write about whether you agree or disagree.

Scoring

Your finished essay will be given to two different essay graders (often English or writing teachers). Each grader is instructed to spend no more than *3 minutes* reading an essay before giving it a score on a scale of 1 to 6. The two scores are then added together to make up your Essay subscore, which ranges from 2 to 12. (If two graders give wildly different scores to the same essay, like a 2 and a 5, a third grader is brought in.) Your Essay score is then combined with your Writing multiple-choice subscore to produce your overarching SAT Writing score.

The graders know you only have 25 minutes. And now you know the people grading it spend all of 3 minutes reading it. So forget about trying to write an essay that changes the world. Write a good first draft that's free of major errors and gives the graders exactly what they want, and you'll do fine.

ESSENTIAL CONCEPTS

When the test makers say to you, "Here's 25 minutes, write an essay," what they're *really* saying is, "Write a *standard* essay that does exactly what we want." The different grades from 1 to 6 are based on the quality of your essay in four areas:

1. Positioning
2. Examples
3. Organization
4. Command of Language

Essential Concept #1: Positioning

Essay graders will be looking for the strength and clarity of your stance, or *position*, on the given topic. You need to take a strong position. To do that, you should always:

- **Rephrase the prompt.** Make the prompt more specific and intelligible by putting it into your own words. In addition to narrowing down the focus of the original, broad topic, rephrasing it enables you to take a position confidently because you'll be proving your own statement rather than the more obscure version put forth by the SAT.
- **Choose your position.** Agree or disagree with it, but be clear about which side you're on. You may be tempted to switch positions or argue both sides. Don't do that. Instead, keep it simple.

Essential Concept #2: Examples

Excellent examples make an SAT Essay shine. You'll use your examples to develop and support your position on the topic. Endeavor to make your examples specific and varied.

BE SPECIFIC

Just as bricks hold up a building, detailed examples support an argument. There are literally millions of good, potential examples for every position you might choose. Choose examples that you know a lot about in order to be specific. Knowing a lot about an example means you know more than just the basic facts. You need to be able to use all the detailed facts about your example, such as dates and events, to show how your example proves your argument.

For example, say you wanted to use an example from the American Revolution to support the position that "learning the lessons taught by failure is a sure route to success." To make your example really great, you have to write more than just, "The American army learned from its mistakes and defeated the British." Instead, you need to include info about battles and tactics. You might discuss the Treaty of Paris, signed in 1783, which officially granted Americans independence and gave the United States all lands east of the Mississippi River.

If you pick an example from your personal life, it doesn't even have to be true or have actually happened. It just needs to support your argument. Don't make up wild stories, but don't worry about stretching the truth a little bit. The essay graders won't know.

BE VARIED

You're more likely to impress the essay grader if you use a broad range of examples from different areas, such as history, art, politics, literature, or science.

To prove the position that "there's no success like failure," you might choose one example each from history, literature, business or current events, and personal experience. Here are some examples that you might choose from these areas:

- **History:** Weak Articles of Confederation led to stronger U.S. Constitution
- **Literature:** Dickens's success in writing about the working class based on his years spent in poverty as a child laborer
- **Business or Current Events:** Google succeeding by learning from the mistakes of its competitors and predecessors
- **Personal Experience:** Your uncle Dave Johnson started a business after getting fired

---

A broad array of examples like these will provide a more solid and defensible position than three examples drawn from personal experience or from just one or two areas.

Essential Concept #3: Organization

No matter what topic you end up writing about, the organization of your essay should be the same. Use this format:

- **Paragraph 1:** Introduction
- **Paragraphs 2–4:** Example Paragraphs
- **Paragraph 5:** Conclusion

Let's look at these paragraphs in detail.

INTRODUCTION

The introduction to an SAT Essay has to do two things:

- Explain your position on the topic clearly and concisely.
- Transition the grader smoothly into your three examples.

To accomplish these goals, you need three to four sentences that convey your thesis statement and the overall map of your essay.

The Thesis Statement. The thesis statement identifies where you stand on the topic and pulls the grader into your essay. A good thesis statement is strong, clear, and definitive. It's often the first sentence of an essay. Here's an example based on the topic "Is there truly no success like failure?":

Learning from the lessons taught by failure is a sure route to success.

The Essay Summary. The rest of your first paragraph should serve as a summary of the examples you will use to support your position on the topic. Explain and describe your three examples to make it clear how they fit into your essay. It's usually best to give about three examples, and each example should get its own sentence. Here's an example of an introductory paragraph:

> The United States of America can be seen as a success that emerged from failure: By learning from the weaknesses of the Articles of Confederation, the founding fathers were able to create the Constitution, the document on which America is built. Google Inc., the popular Internet search engine, is another example of a success that arose from learning from failure, though in this case Google learned from the failures of its competitors. Another example that shows how success can arise from failure is the story of Dave Johnson, who started a recruiting firm that rose out of the ashes of Johnson's personal experience of being laid off.

EXAMPLE PARAGRAPHS

After your introduction come two or three body paragraphs, in which you discuss each of your examples in detail. Each example paragraph should follow this basic format:

- **Sentence 1:** The first sentence should be the *topic sentence*, which serves as the thesis statement of the paragraph. It explains what your example is and places it within the context of your argument.
- **Sentences 2–5:** The next three to four sentences should *develop your example*. In these sentences, you show through specific, concrete discussion of facts and situations just how your example supports your essay's thesis statement.

Here's an example of a body paragraph:

> The United States, the first great democracy of the modern world, is also
> one of the best examples of a success achieved by studying and learning
> from earlier failures. After just five years of living under the Articles of
> Confederation, which established the United States of America as a
> single country for the first time, the states realized that they needed
> a new document and a new, more powerful government. In 1786, the
> Annapolis convention was convened. The result, three years later, was
> the Constitution, which created a more powerful central government
> while also maintaining the integrity of the states. By learning from the
> failure of the Articles, the founding fathers created the founding docu-
> ment of a country that has become both the most powerful country in
> the world and a beacon of democracy.

Transitions Between Example Paragraphs. Your first example paragraph
can dive right into its topic sentence, but the other paragraphs need transitions. The simplest way to build these transitions is to use words like *another*
and *finally*. That means your second example paragraph should start with a
transitional phrase such as *another example*, and your third example paragraph should begin along the lines of *lastly* or *finally*.

CONCLUSION

The conclusion of your essay should recap your argument while also broadening it a bit. By "broadening" your argument, we mean that you should
attempt to link your specific examples to wider fields, such as politics,
business, and art. Here's an example of a conclusion that both recaps and
broadens our argument about failure:

> The examples of the U.S. Constitution, Google, and Dave Johnson make it
> clear that in the realms of politics and business, the greatest successes

arise from careful considerations of the lessons of failure. Failure is often seen as embarrassing, something to be denied and hidden. But as the examples of the U.S. Constitution, Google, and Dave Johnson show, if an individual, an organization, or even a nation is strong enough to face and study its failure, then that failure can become a powerful teacher. As the examples of history and business demonstrate, if everyone had the courage and insight to view failure as a surefire way to learn from mistakes, success would be easier to achieve.

THE UNIVERSAL SAT ESSAY TEMPLATE

The following SAT Essay outline will provide you with a quick at-a-glance summary of the essential components we just discussed. You can use this template no matter what topic you get or position you take:

	LENGTH	PURPOSE
INTRODUCTION		
Thesis Statement	1 sentence	Describe your argument clearly and concisely.
Essay Summary	3 sentences	Lay out the examples you'll use to support your thesis statement.
EXAMPLE PARAGRAPH #1		
Topic Sentence	1 sentence	Describe your example and fit it into the context of your overall thesis statement.
Example Development	3–4 sentences	Use specific facts to show how your example supports your argument. Be as specific as possible.

EXAMPLE PARAGRAPH #2

Topic Sentence	1 sentence	Describe your example and fit it into the context of your overall thesis statement.
Example Development	3–4 sentences	Use specific facts to show how your example supports your argument. Be as specific as possible.

EXAMPLE PARAGRAPH #3

Topic Sentence	1 sentence	Describe your example and fit it into the context of your overall thesis statement.
Example Development	3–4 sentences	Use specific facts to show how your example supports your argument. Be as specific as possible.

CONCLUSION

Recap	1 sentence	Summarize your argument and examples.
Broaden	2–3 sentences	Expand your position by showing how your argument relates to other topics like politics or art, or by contemplating what would happen in the world if people (or nations or businesses) followed the argument you make in your essay.

Essential Concept #4:
Command of Language

SAT essay graders care about the mechanics of your writing. That said, there's not enough time to re-invent your writing style before test day. Instead, focus on these elements of good writing:

- Variation in Sentence Structure
- Transitions
- Grammar and Spelling

VARIATION IN SENTENCE STRUCTURE

Here's an example of boring, repetitive sentence structure:

> Sentence structure, if done well, can keep your readers engaged and help make your essay exciting and easier to read. Sentence structure, if it is monotonous and unchanging, can make your essay sound boring and unsophisticated. Sentence structure is important on the SAT Essay. Sentence structure is also important in essays you write for school.

Changing the rhythm of the writing can make it more interesting.

> Sentence structure is very important. Varying the structure of your sentences keeps your reader engaged and makes your writing easier to read and more exciting. Monotonous and repetitive sentence structure can make your essay sound boring and unsophisticated. Mixing up your sentence structure is crucial on the SAT Essay—it's also important to consider when writing essays for school.

You don't have to invert every clause, but you should be careful not to let more than a few sentences in a row follow the same exact structure.

TRANSITIONS

One great way to vary your sentence structure while improving the logical flow of your essay is to use transitions. Here are some different kinds of transitions you can use to spice up your sentence structure:

- **Showing Contrast:** Katie likes pink nail polish. *In contrast*, she thinks red nail polish looks trashy.
- **Elaborating:** I love sneaking into movies. *Even more than that*, I love trying to steal candy while I'm there.
- **Providing an Example:** If you save up your money, you can afford pricey items. *For example*, Patrick saved up his allowance and eventually purchased a sports car.
- **Showing Results:** Manuel ingested nothing but soda and burgers every day for a month. *As a result*, he gained ten pounds.
- **Showing Sequence:** The police arrested Bob at the party. *Soon after*, his college applications were all rejected, and eventually Bob drifted into a life of crime.

GRAMMAR AND SPELLING

A few grammar or spelling mistakes in your essay will not destroy your score. The essay graders understand that you're bound to make minor mistakes in a rushed 25-minute essay. Instead, graders are instructed to look out for patterns of errors. If a grader sees that your punctuation is consistently wrong, that your spelling of familiar words is often incorrect, or that you write run-on sentences again and again, your score will suffer.

If you need a grammar brush up, take a look at the grammar errors covered in Intensive 2. There we cover the Writing Section's multiple-choice questions and show you how to identify sentence and paragraph errors. As you'll see, many of these questions test your understanding of proper grammar. Once you know what they look like, you can avoid them in your own writing. As for spelling, your best bet is to stick with familiar words. The SAT Essay isn't the time to try out fancy vocabulary.

ESSENTIAL STRATEGY

Now let's turn our attention to the step method you should use for your SAT Essay, no matter what topic the test makers throw at you:

Step 1: Understand the topic and take a position (1 minute).

Step 2: Brainstorm examples (2–3 minutes).

Step 3: Create an outline (3–4 minutes).

Step 4: Write the essay (15 minutes).

Step 5: Proof the essay (2 minutes).

We've noted how much time you should spend on each step. Remember that you'll have only 25 minutes to plan, draft, and proofread your essay.

Step 1: Understand the topic and take a position (1 minute). Before you can even think about writing the Essay you must read the prompt very carefully. Make sure you understand it thoroughly by rephrasing the prompt and choosing your position. Remember: No matter how polished your essay may be, if you don't write *on topic,* you'll get zero points!

Step 2: Brainstorm examples (2–3 minutes). Suppose your position is that you agree with the statement "failure can lead to success by teaching important lessons that help us avoid repeating mistakes in the future." *Brainstorming*, or thinking up examples to support your position, is the crucial next step. Skipping this step will leave you with a position but no examples. You'll write the first thing that comes to mind, and your essay will probably derail. The best examples you can generate to support your SAT Essay will come from a variety of sources, such as science, history, politics, art, literature, business, and personal experience. So brainstorm a list split up by category. List your categories and then see what you come up with.

Once you've got a list, pick your top three examples. To decide among them, ask yourself three questions:

- Which examples can I be most specific about?
- Which examples will give my essay the broadest range?
- Which examples are controversial? (Avoid those.)

Step 3: Create an outline (3–4 minutes). The SAT Essay rewards standard conformity much more than it does creativity. Organizing your ideas in outline form and then sticking to that outline is crucial. We guarantee that the 3 or 4 minutes you invest in this step will definitely be paid back when you write your essay. Take a look at our Universal SAT Essay Template to see what your essay should contain.

As you sketch out your outline, consider where you want each example to go. Put your strongest example first, followed by the second strongest, and then the least strong. Here's a sample outline based on the examples we've been using throughout this Intensive:

PARAGRAPH 1: INTRODUCTION	Failure can lead to success teaching lessons, learning mistakes. Three examples: (1) U.S. Constitution after Articles' failure, (2) failed dot-coms lead to more successful online businesses, (3) guy who started successful recruiting business after getting laid off.
PARAGRAPH 2: EXAMPLE 1 (BEST)	U.S. Constitution developed by studying the failures of previous document, Articles of Confederation. By studying failures, U.S. became true revolutionary democracy.
PARAGRAPH 3: EXAMPLE 2 (NEXT BEST)	Google studied competitors' struggles, came up with better technological solution and better business model. Because failure is good teacher, intelligent companies look for failure everywhere, even in rivals, to learn and evolve.
PARAGRAPH 4: EXAMPLE 3 (NEXT BEST)	Johnson founded job placement agency based on difficulties finding a new job after getting laid off. Studied his failure, found problems lay with system, not with him.
PARAGRAPH 5: CONCLUSION	Failure often seen as embarrassing. People try to hide it. But if you or society take responsibility for it, study it, history shows failure leads to success for everyone.

Your outline doesn't have to be written in complete sentences. Feel free to write just enough to convey to yourself what you need to follow during the actual writing of your essay. Once you have the outline down on paper, Step 4 becomes more a job of polishing language and ideas than of creating them from scratch.

Step 4: **Write the essay (15 minutes)**. Writing the essay consists of filling out your ideas by following your outline and plugging in what's missing. That adds up to only about ten more sentences than what you've jotted down in your outline, which should already contain a basic version of your thesis statement, one topic sentence for each of your three examples, and a conclusion statement that ties everything together.

If you're running out of time before finishing the intro, example paragraphs, and conclusion, drop one of your example paragraphs. You can still get a decent score. Just be sure to include an introduction and a conclusion.

Step 5: **Proof the essay (2 minutes)**. Proofing your essay means reading through your finished essay to correct mistakes or to clear up words that are difficult to read. If you don't have 2 minutes after you've finished writing the essay (Step 4), spend whatever time you do have left proofing. Read over your essay and search for rough writing, bad transitions, grammatical errors, and repetitive sentence structure. The SAT explicitly states that handwriting will not affect your grade, but you should also be on the lookout for instances in which bad handwriting makes it look as if you've made a grammatical or spelling mistake.

The Finished Essay: Our Example

Here's a sample SAT Essay. As you'll see, it draws on the examples we've been discussing throughout this Intensive.

Learning the lessons taught by failure is a sure route to success. (THESIS STATEMENT) The United States of America can be seen as a success that emerged from failure: by learning from the weaknesses of the Articles of Confederation, the founding fathers were able to create the Constitution, the document on which America is built. (BEST SUPPORTING EXAMPLE [1]) Google Inc., the popular Internet search engine, is another example of a success that arose from learning from failure, though in this case Google learned from the failures of its competitors. (NEXT BEST SUPPORTING EXAMPLE [2]) Another example that shows how success can arise from failure is the story of Dave Johnson, who started a recruiting firm that arose from Johnson's personal experience of being laid off. (NEXT BEST SUPPORTING EXAMPLE [3])

The United States, the first great democracy of the modern world, is also one of the best examples of a success achieved by studying and learning from earlier failures. (TOPIC SENTENCE FOR EXAMPLE 1) After just five years of living under the Articles of Confederation, which established the United States of America as a single country for the first time, the states realized that they needed a new document and a new, more powerful government. In 1786, the Annapolis convention was convened. The result, three years later, was the Constitution, which created a more powerful central government while also maintaining the integrity of the states. By learning from the failure of the Articles, the founding fathers created the founding document of a country that has become both the most powerful country in the world and a beacon of democracy. (DEVELOPMENT SENTENCES TO SUPPORT EXAMPLE 1)

Unlike the United States, which had its fair share of ups and downs over the years, the Internet search engine company, Google, has suffered few setbacks since it went into business in the late 1990s. (TOPIC SENTENCE FOR EXAMPLE 2) Google has succeeded by studying the failures of other companies in order to help it innovate its technology and business model. Google identified and solved the problem of assessing the quality of search results by using the number of links pointing to a page as an indicator of the number of people who find the page valuable. Suddenly, Google's search results became far more accurate and reliable than those from other companies, and now Google's dominance in the field of Internet search is absolute. (DEVELOPMENT SENTENCES TO SUPPORT EXAMPLE 2)

The example of Dave Johnson's success also shows how effective learning from mistakes and failure can be. (TOPIC SENTENCE FOR EXAMPLE 3) Rather than accept his failure after being laid off, Johnson decided to study it. After a month of research, Johnson realized that his failure to find a new job resulted primarily from the inefficiency of the local job placement agencies, not from his own deficiencies. A month later, Johnson created Johnson Staffing to correct this weakness in the job placement sector. Today Johnson Staffing is the largest job placement agency in South Carolina and is in the process of expanding into a national corporation. (DEVELOPMENT SENTENCES TO SUPPORT EXAMPLE 3)

    Failure is often seen as embarrassing, something to be denied and hidden. But as the examples of the U.S. Constitution, Google, and Dave Johnson prove, if an individual, organization, or even a nation is strong enough to face and study its failure, then that failure can become a powerful teacher. (THESIS STATEMENT REPHRASED IN A BROADER WAY THAT PUSHES IT FURTHER) The examples of history and business demonstrate that failure can be the best catalyst of success, but only if people have the courage to face it head on.

WHY THIS ESSAY DESERVES A "6"

This essay shows mastery of all four Essential Concepts: *positioning, examples, organization,* and *command of language.* It takes a very strong and clear stance on the topic in the first sentence and sticks to it from start to finish. It uses three examples from a very diverse array of disciplines— from history and politics to Internet technology to a profile of an entrepreneur—and it never veers from using these examples to support the thesis statement's position. At the same time, the examples are specific, with dates and facts sprinkled throughout each paragraph.

The organization of the essay follows our standard SAT Essay format both at the paragraph level (topic sentences and development sentences) and at the overall essay level (intro, three meaty example paragraphs, a strong conclusion). The command of language remains solid throughout. The writer does not take risks with unfamiliar vocabulary but instead chooses a few out-of-the-ordinary words like *beacon, deficiencies,* and *catalyst.* Sentence structure varies often, making the entire essay more interesting and engaging to the grader. Finally, no significant grammar errors disrupt the overall excellence of this SAT Essay.

Now that you know what to do, the next step is to try it out on a practice topic.

PRACTICE SET

Plan, write, and score your response to the prompt that follows, based on our Universal SAT Essay Template. Remember you'll have just 25 minutes on test day.

Think carefully about the issue presented in the following excerpt and the assignment below.

An old proverb states that "Knowledge in youth is wisdom in age." Some take this saying to mean that the education one acquires throughout youth only becomes wisdom over time, as one ages and broadens his or her experience. Others view the proverb as a dismissal of the notion that only the aged and experienced can ever be truly wise.

Assignment:

Does education acquired throughout youth translate to wisdom, or are only the aged and experienced truly wise? Plan and write an essay in which you develop your point of view on this issue. Support your position with reasoning and examples taken from your reading, studies, experience, or observations.

Guided Explanations

A "6" ESSAY

It is not always true that wisdom only comes with age because children and young people often demonstrate wisdom. You can see this in Henry James's novel *What Maisie Knew*; you can also find it in Martin Amis's novel *The Rachel Papers*. Finally, there is the example of Bobby Fischer, a chess prodigy who astounded players worldwide by beating even the most experienced adult chess players. In all of these examples, young people demonstrate wisdom beyond their years.

What Maisie Knew is about a very young yet wise girl whose parents are in the process of a messy, acrimonious divorce. Throughout the novel, Maisie perceives human relationships with a much keener and kinder eye than the adults around her. James points out that it is not the ability to grasp the concepts of divorce and alimony and adultery that makes someone wise: Its the ability to understand people's behavior. Maisie senses every twitch and change in mood in everyone around her, and its this ability that makes her wise beyond her years.

The Rachel Papers stars a teenage character named Charles who demonstrates more wisdom than any of the adults around him. He examines his human relationships in a way that eludes his own father. Charles is extremely concerned with treating people with kindness, whereas his father cheats on Charles's mother and finds nothing wrong with his infidelity. Charles makes close notes of every important conversation he has with his family, and studies his papers for clues to their significance—just another sign of his maturity and wisdom.

Bobby Fischer became a grandmaster of chess at age fifteen. The young Fischer astounded even the most seasoned chess players starting at age 12 when he first joined the Manhattan Chess Club, where the best players in the world square off. Fischer's success was bolstered by his strong IQ and amazing memory, both of which helped him routinely defeat adults many times his age.

The young characters in the novels of Henry James and Martin Amis show their readers a different kind of wisdom—a thoughtfulness and insight into human relations that young people possess, and older people can lack. The example of Bobby Fischer proves that children can possess intellectual capabilities that rival or even exceed those of adults. If everyone swore off the notion that "With age comes wisdom," young people would be empowered to have much more of an impact on the world.

On page 48 is a quick checklist that shows how this essay stacks up against our criteria for our Universal SAT Essay Template.

OUR UNIVERSAL SAT ESSAY TEMPLATE CRITERIA	YES OR NO?
Thesis statement in first sentence of paragraph 1	YES
Three examples listed in paragraph 1 in order from best to worst	YES
Topic sentence for example in paragraph 2	YES
3–4 development sentences to support paragraph 2's example	YES
Topic sentence for example in paragraph 3	YES
3–4 development sentences to support paragraph 3's example	YES
Topic sentence for example in paragraph 4	YES
3–4 development sentences to support paragraph 4's example	YES
Conclusion paragraph contains rephrased and broadened thesis statement	YES

Let's take a closer look at the essay based on our four Essential Concepts: positioning, organization, examples, and command of language.

Positioning. The writer takes a strong and clear stance on the essay topic right from the start. The first sentence contains a thesis statement, and the first paragraph spells out the three examples the she will use to support her position: two from literature (Henry James and Martin Amis) and one from recent history (Bobby Fischer).

Examples. The writer spells out the three examples she will use to prove the position on the topic. In this case, the writer takes the position that the phrase "With age comes wisdom" is disproved by the existence of many examples of exceptionally "wise" young people. To prove it, the writer uses three diverse examples: one from a Henry James novel (*What Maisie Knew*), one from a Martin Amis novel (*The Rachel Papers*), and one from recent history (Bobby Fischer). The writer could have chosen a more diverse mix of examples to impress the grader with a greater breadth of knowledge. Even so, because the writer uses these examples so effectively to prove the thesis statement, any grader would likely not deduct points due to the examples' lack of breadth.

Organization. The writer organizes this essay based precisely on the structure we suggest in our Universal SAT Essay Template. The essay contains five paragraphs of at least three sentences each. The paragraphs are organized into an introduction, three example paragraphs starting with the strongest example, and a conclusion that sums up and broadens the argument.

Command of Language. As this essay proves, "6" essays can have errors. In fact, SAT essay graders should expect at least a few errors in every SAT essay. This essay contains a few minor slips regarding the writer's command of language, such as the misspelling *its* instead of *it's*. This sentence includes a faulty comparison: "Maisie sees human relationships with a much keener and kinder eye than the adults around her." This comparison suggests that Maisie sees relationships more clearly than she sees adults; what the writer means to suggest, however, is that Maisie sees relationships more clearly than adults see relationships. Overall, the errors in this essay are minor and few, nothing substantial enough to result in a lower score.

A few flashes of impressive vocabulary combined with appropriate word choice give this essay just enough pizzazz to convey the writer's strong command of language. The writer also varies the sentence structure frequently, making the essay interesting and easy to read. One exception is the writer's repeated use of the word *wisdom*. It's obviously tough to limit the use of this word because it appears in the prompt. Still, the writer's command of language would have been even more impressive if the writer had used a synonym, such as *astuteness*.

INTENSIVE 2

Writing Section:
Multiple-Choice Questions

Multiple-Choice Questions X-ray

Essential Concepts

Essential Strategies

Practice Set

IN TOTAL, THE WRITING SECTION HAS 49 MULTIPLE-CHOICE questions in two timed sections. There are three question types:

- Identifying Sentence Errors (18 questions)
- Improving Sentences (25 questions)
- Improving Paragraphs (6 questions)

Your performance on these questions, combined with how well you do on the Essay, forms your SAT Writing score.

The Writing Section's multiple-choice questions test your understanding of grammar and language usage. Mastering them doesn't require you to memorize a huge amount of material or learn a ton of new concepts, however. In fact, you probably already know how to identify sentence errors and improve sentences and paragraphs, even if you don't recognize the names of some of the grammar rules we discuss in this Intensive. Let's first start with an X-ray and get familiar with the question types.

MULTIPLE-CHOICE QUESTIONS X-RAY

We'll spend this section looking at the Writing Section's three types of multiple-choice questions in detail. Review the directions so that you can spend less of your time with them on test day.

Identifying Sentence Errors

Directions for Identifying Sentence Errors: The sentences that follow assess whether you can recognize grammatical and usage errors. Every sentence is either grammatically correct or has one and only one error. If there is an error, the error will be lettered and underlined. Select the underlined part that must be fixed in order to make the sentence correct and error free. If the sentence is correct and error-free, choose E.

<u>Even though</u> Esther created a petition to protest the <u>crowning</u> of a prom
    A   B

queen, <u>there is</u> many people who refused to sign, saying they support the
       C

<u>1950s-era</u> tradition. <u>No error</u>
   D   E

There are two subtle points to understand about Identifying Sentence Errors: First, follow the requirements of standard written English. That means, "Hello, how are you?" instead of "Hey, what's up?"

Second, the directions tell you that some of the sentences are completely correct. Choice **E** will always mean that the sentence is fine as it is. Expect roughly 20 percent of Identifying Sentence Errors to not have any errors. That means you shouldn't be alarmed if you can't find an error, because it will happen in one out of every five questions. By the way, the answer to our sample question is **C**; we'll show you why later in this Intensive.

Improving Sentences

Directions for Improving Sentences: The sentences that follow assess whether you can identify and correct grammatical and usage errors, as well as recognize sentences that correctly adhere to the rules of standard written English.

A part of a sentence or the entire sentence will be underlined. Answers B–E consist of new ways of stating the underlined material; answer A is the same as the original sentence. Choose A if the original sentence is correct and produces the most effective sentence. Otherwise, choose one of the other answers.

In choosing answers, follow the requirements of standard written English and consider pay attention to grammar, choice of words, sentence construction, and punctuation. Your answer should create the best sentence—clear and precise, without awkwardness or ambiguity.

Eager to pass his final exams, studying was the student's top priority.

(A) studying was the student's top priority.
(B) the student made studying his top priority.
(C) the top priority of the student was studying.
(D) the student's top priority was studying.
(E) studying was the top priority for the student.

Once again, the SAT wants you to follow the rules of standard *written* English. The rules of standard *spoken* English aren't accepted here, so a lot of English that's passable in speech is considered incorrect on Improving Sentences questions.

These questions ask you to choose the answer that best improves the sentence. Note that **A** reproduces the underlined portion of the question. **A** is essentially Improving Sentence's "No error" choice. Because **A** is always the same as the original sentence, *you never have to waste time reading* **A**. Expect roughly 20 percent of Improving Sentences to not need any improvement. So, unless you think the sentence contains no error, skip directly to **B**. Here, the correct answer is **D**.

Improving Paragraphs

(1) Japanese cuisine continues to grow in popularity in the United States.
(2) Americans are already fond of Chinese food. (3) Now they are discovering
that Japanese cuisine takes a similar set of basic ingredients and transforms
them into something quite special. (4) That Japanese food is generally low in
fat and calories, and offers many options for vegetarians and vegans, adds to its
popularity.

(5) Americans' enjoyment of Japanese cooking is still largely limited to an
occasional night out at a Japanese restaurant. (6) Actually, Japanese cooking
is surprisingly simple. (7) Anyone with a standard set of cooking utensils and
knowledge of basic cooking terms can easily follow the recipes in any Japanese
cookbook.

(8) Since Japanese restaurants tend to be fairly expensive, one would think
that fans of the cuisine would be excited about the possibility of making it
at home. (9) Unfortunately, many traditional Japanese recipes call for costly
ingredients that often can only be found at Asian grocery stores. (10) As these
ingredients become more widely available at lower prices, we are sure to see a
proportional increase in the number of people cooking Japanese food at home.

In context, what is the best way to revise and combine sentences 2 and 3 (reproduced below)?

Americans are already fond of Chinese food. Now they are discovering that Japanese cuisine takes a similar set of basic ingredients and transforms them into something quite special.

(A) American people are already fond of Chinese food, and have discovered that Japanese cuisine takes a similar set of basic ingredients and transforms them into something quite special.

(B) American people are already fond of Chinese food, and now discover that Japanese cuisine takes a similar set of basic ingredients and transforms them into something quite special.

(C) Already fond of Chinese food, American people are now discovering that Japanese cuisine takes a similar set of basic ingredients and transforms them into something quite special.

(D) Already fond of Chinese food, having discovered that Japanese cuisine takes a similar set of basic ingredients and transforms them into something quite special, American people like it.

(E) American people are already fond of Chinese food; however, they are discovering that Japanese cuisine takes a similar set of basic ingredients and transforms them into something quite special.

As with Improving Sentences, Improving Paragraph questions ask you to choose the answer that best improves a paragraph or portion of the paragraph. These questions present you with a rough draft of an essay. Some questions will ask you to fix or combine individual sentences, and some will address the essay as a whole. Note again the SAT's emphasis on standard written English. The correct answer is **C**.

ESSENTIAL CONCEPTS

Although the multiple-choice question types vary in structure, they all test your understanding of the following concepts:

1. Punctuation
2. Basic Grammar and Usage
3. Sentence Structure

Essential Concept #1: Punctuation

Punctuation is the set of marks that shows you how to read and understand sentences. Many Identifying Sentence Errors and Improving Sentences questions will test punctuation, including the following:

- Commas
- Semicolons
- Colons

COMMAS

Misplaced, misused, and missing commas are the most frequent punctuation offenders on the SAT's Writing section. Here's how commas work:

Commas Separate Independent Clauses Joined by a Conjunction. An independent clause contains a subject and a verb (an independent clause can be as short as *I am* or *he reads*), and it can function as a sentence on its own. When you see a conjunction (*and, but, for, or, nor, so, yet*) joining independent clauses, a comma should precede the conjunction. For example:

An independent clause contains a subject and a verb, *and* it can function as a sentence on its own.

Lesley wanted to sit outside, *but* it was raining.

Henry could tie the shoe himself, *or* he could ask Amanda to tie his shoe.

In each example, the clauses on both sides of the comma could stand as sentences on their own. With the addition of the comma and conjunction, the two independent clauses become one sentence.

Commas Delineate a Series of Items. A series contains three or more items separated by commas. The items in a series can be either nouns (such as *dog*) or verb phrases (such as *get in the car*). Commas are essentially the structural backbone of a series. For example:

The hungry girl devoured *a chicken, two pounds of pasta, and a chocolate cake.*

When he learned his girlfriend was coming over, *Nathaniel took a shower, brushed his teeth, and cleaned his room.*

The comma follows all but the last item in the series. When using a conjunction, such as *and* or *or*, at the end of the series, remember to precede it with a comma *(. . . brushed his teeth, **and** cleaned his room)*.

Commas Set Off Dependent Phrases and Clauses from the Main Clause of a Sentence. Unlike independent clauses, dependent phrases and clauses are not sentences in themselves; rather, they serve to explain or embellish the main clause of a sentence. When they appear at the beginning of a sentence, they should be set off from the main clause by a comma. For example:

Scared of monsters, Tina always checked under her bed before going to sleep.

After preparing an elaborate meal for herself, Anne was too tired to eat.

The first example shows a dependent clause (*Scared of monsters*) acting as an adjective modifying *Tina.* The second example shows a dependent clause acting as an adverb.

Since the adverbial clause is at the beginning of the sentence, it needs to be set off from the main clause by a comma. Adverbial clauses should also be set off by commas if they appear in the middle of a sentence. However, if an adverbial clause appears at the end of a sentence, you do not need to use a comma. For example:

Anne was too tired to eat *after preparing an elaborate meal for herself.*

Commas Set Off Nonessential Phrases and Clauses. Nonessential phrases embellish nouns without specifying them. Nonessential phrases should be set off from the rest of the sentence by commas. For example:

Everyone voted Carrie, *who is the most popular girl in our class,* prom queen.

The decrepit street sign, *which had stood in our town since 1799,* finally fell down.

When you use nonessential phrases like the two above, you assume that *Carrie* and *the decrepit street sign* do not need any further identification. If you remove the nonessential phrases, you should still be able to understand the sentences.

Restrictive phrases, however, are *not* set off by commas because they are necessary to understand the modified noun and the sentence as a whole. For example:

The girl *who is sick* missed three days of school.

The dog *that ate the rotten steak* fell down.

If you removed the restrictive phrases (*who is sick* and *that ate the rotten steak*) from these sentences, you would be left wondering "which girl?" and "which dog?" These restrictive phrases are used to identify exactly which girl missed school and exactly which dog fell. Setting off *who is sick* in commas would assume that the girl's identity is never in doubt—there is only one girl who could have missed school. In the example, though, we know the identity of the girl only because the restrictive phrase specifies *the girl who is sick*.

Commas Set Off Appositives. Appositives are similar to nonessential phrases. An appositive is a phrase that renames or restates the modified noun, usually enhancing it with additional information. For example:

Everyone voted Carrie, *the most popular girl in school,* prom queen.

The dog, *a Yorkshire terrier,* barked at all the neighbors.

In these two examples, *the most popular girl in school* and *a Yorkshire terrier* are appositives used to describe the nouns they modify.

SEMICOLONS

Use a semicolon when you need to join related independent clauses.

Semicolons are commonly used to separate two related but independent clauses. For example:

Julie ate five brownies; Eileen ate seven.

Josh needed to buy peas; he ran to the market.

In these cases, you can think of the semicolon as a *weak period*. It suggests a short pause before moving on to a related thought, whereas a period suggests a full stop before moving on to a less-related thought. Generally, a period between these independent clauses would work just as well as a semicolon, so the SAT answer choices won't offer you a choice between period or semicolon. But you may see the semicolon employed as a weak period in an answer choice; in that case, you should know that it is being used correctly.

Frequently, you will see two independent clauses joined by a semicolon and a transitional adverb (such as *consequently, however, furthermore, indeed, moreover, nevertheless, therefore*, and *thus*). For example:

Julie ate five brownies; *however,* Eileen ate seven.

Josh needed to buy peas; *therefore,* he ran to the market.

If you can't go to the prom with me, let me know as soon as possible; *otherwise,* I'll resent you and your inability to communicate for the rest of my life.

Most transitional adverbs should be followed by a comma, but for short adverbs, such as *thus*, the comma can be omitted. If you see a transitional adverb on its own or preceded by a comma on the SAT, you should immediately know there's an error.

COLONS

Colons are used after complete sentences to introduce related information that usually comes in the form of a list, an explanation, or a quotation. When you see a colon, you should know to expect elaborating information. Avoid making mistakes with colons by following these two rules:

1. A colon should always be preceded by an independent clause.

Incorrect: The ingredients I need to make a cake: flour, butter, sugar, and icing.

Correct: I need several ingredients to make a cake: flour, butter, sugar, and icing.

In the incorrect example, a sentence fragment precedes the list. The sentence should be reworked to create an independent clause before the colon.

2. There should never be more than one colon in a sentence.

Incorrect: He brought many items on the camping trip: a tent, a sleeping bag, a full cooking set, warm clothes, and several pairs of shoes: sneakers, boots, and sandals.

Correct: He brought many items on the camping trip: a tent, a sleeping bag, a full cooking set, warm clothes, sneakers, boots, and sandals.

If you see a sentence that contains more than one colon or lists within lists, the sentence needs to be rephrased.

Essential Concept # 2:
Basic Grammar and Usage

Many questions will test your understanding of the rules of basic grammar and usage. The following are the ones that you'll likely encounter on the Writing section:

- Subject-Verb Agreement
- Pronoun-Antecedent Agreement
- Noun-Number Agreement
- Pronoun Cases
- Verb Tense

SUBJECT-VERB AGREEMENT

Singular verbs must accompany singular subjects, and plural verbs must accompany plural subjects. Take a look at these examples:

Singular: The *man wears four* ties.

His favorite *college is* in Nebraska.

Matt, along with his friends, *goes* to Coney Island.

Plural: The *men wear* four ties each.

His favorite *colleges are* in Nebraska.

Matt and his friends go to Coney Island.

In the first example with Matt, the subject is singular because the phrase *along with his friends* is isolated in commas. But in the second example with Matt, his friends join the action; the subject becomes *Matt and his friends*, calling for the change to a plural verb.

Subject-verb agreement is fairly straightforward, but the SAT may make this concept tricky. Knowing the different ways subjects and verbs can go astray will help you on test day. We'll show you how in the context of several Identifying Sentence Error questions.

Subject After the Verb. In most sentences, the subject comes before the verb. The SAT tries to throw you off by giving you a sentence or two in which the subject comes *after* the verb, and the subject-verb match-up is incorrect.

<u>Even though</u> Esther created a petition to protest the <u>crowning</u> of a prom queen,
   A   B
<u>there is</u> many people who refused to sign, saying they support the <u>1950s-era</u>
   C   D
tradition. <u>No error</u>
              E

The SAT frequently uses this exact formulation, so be wary if you see a comma followed by the word *there*. In this kind of sentence, it's tempting to assume that just because the word *there* comes before the verb *is, there* is the subject—but it's not. *People* is the subject. And because *people* is plural, the matching verb also must be plural. *Is* is a singular verb, and therefore incorrect in this sentence.

Even when you don't see the red flag of *there is,* don't just assume that the subject always comes before the verb. Look at the following sentence:

Atop my sundae, a colossal <u>mass</u> of ice cream, <u>whipped cream</u>, and sprinkles, <u>sits</u>
    A   B   C   D

two maraschino cherries. <u>No error</u>
                                      E

Tricky! The answer is D, sits. Because the things doing the sitting are *two maraschino cherries* (plural subject), you need to use sit (plural verb). The sentence should read Atop my sundae, a colossal mass of ice cream, whipped cream, and sprinkles, sit two maraschino cherries. Why is this so sneaky? The subject, maraschino cherries, comes after the verb, sits. With all the singular stuff floating around—one sundae, one mass of ice cream and whipped cream—it's easy to assume that the verb should be singular too. Look out for that kind of backward construction.

Subject and Verb Are Separated. One of the SAT's most diabolical tricks is to put the subject here and the verb *waaaaay* over yonder. The test writers hope that by the time you get to the verb, you'll forget the subject and end up baffled.

Sundaes with whipped cream and cherries, <u>while</u> good <u>if consumed</u> in
                                                        A   B

moderation, <u>is heinous</u> if eaten <u>for breakfast</u>, lunch, and dinner. <u>No error</u>
                  C   D   E

In this sentence, the subject (*sundaes*) is at the beginning of the sentence, while the verb (*is*) is miles away. When this happens, it's helpful to bracket clauses that separate the subject and the verb so that you can still see how the subject and verb should relate. If you ignore the phrase here (*while good if consumed in moderation*), you're left with *sundaes is heinous*. That's grammatically heinous. So C is the right answer.

Neither/Nor *and* Either/Or. In *neither/nor* and *either/or* constructions, you're always talking about two things, so it's tempting to assume that you always need a plural verb.

But if the two things being discussed are singular, you need a singular verb. For example, it's correct to say *Neither Jason nor Sandra acts well* because if you broke the components of the sentence in two, you would get *Jason acts well* and *Sandra acts well*. It's incorrect to say *Neither Jason or Sandra act well* because if you break that sentence into its components, you get *Jason act well* and *Sandra act well*.

It can be hard to hear this error, so be sure to check subject-verb match-ups carefully when you see a sentence like this one:

Neither Kylie nor Jason measure up to Carrie. No error
A   B   C   D   E

Even though the sentence mentions two people (Jason and Kylie) who don't measure up to Carrie, both of those people are singular nouns. Therefore, the verb must be singular. *Measure* is a plural verb, when it should be a singular one, so C is the answer.

Tricky Singular Subjects That Seem Plural. There are a bunch of confusing subjects out there that are singular but masquerade as plural. It's easy to get tripped up by these singular subjects and mistakenly match them with plural verbs. Here are the leading culprits:

anybody	audience	everyone	none
anyone	each	group	no one
America	either	neither	number
amount	everybody	nobody	

In this sentence, for example, *nobody* seems plural:

> Of all of the <u>students</u> in my class, nobody, not <u>even me</u>, <u>are</u> excited about
>   A   B   C
>
> <u>the new teacher.</u> <u>No error</u>
>   D   E

Nobody is always a singular noun, so it needs to be matched with a singular verb. The answer is C. The sentence should read *Of all the students in my class, nobody, not even me, is excited about the new teacher.* Look carefully at all seemingly plural subjects to make sure they're not singular subjects masquerading as plural ones.

Be particularly careful with phrases like *as well as*, *along with*, and *in addition to*. Like the *neither/nor* construction, these phrases can trick you into thinking they require a plural verb.

> The leadoff hitter, <u>as well as</u> the cleanup hitter, <u>are</u> getting some <u>good</u> hits <u>tonight.</u>
>   A   B   C   D
>
> <u>No error</u>
>   E

The actual subject here is *leadoff hitter*. Because *leadoff hitter* is a singular subject, the verb must be singular too. The presence of the phrase *as well as* does *not* make the subject plural. Even though there are two hitters doing well, the leadoff hitter is the only subject of this sentence. B is the answer; the sentence should read *The leadoff hitter, as well as the cleanup hitter, is getting some good hits tonight.* If the sentence used *and* instead of *as well as*, so that it read *The leadoff hitter and the cleanup hitter are getting some good hits tonight*, then *are* would be correct. It's that *as well as* construction that changes things.

Indefinite Pronouns. Indefinite pronouns refer to persons or things that have not been specified. Matching indefinite pronouns with the correct verb form can be tough. Some indefinite pronouns that seem plural are actually singular. Questions dealing with singular indefinite pronouns are popular with the test makers, so you'd be wise to memorize a few of these pronouns now. The following indefinite pronouns are *always* singular, and they tend to appear a lot on the SAT:

another	each	nobody
anybody	everybody	no one
anyone	everyone	somebody
anything	everything	someone

All the indefinite pronouns in the list above should be followed by singular verbs. For example:

Anyone over the age of 21 *is* eligible to vote in the United States.

Each has its own patch of grass.

If you're used to thinking these pronouns take plural verbs, these sentences probably sound weird to you. Your best bet is to memorize the list above to remember that those pronouns take singular verbs.

You should also be aware that not all indefinite pronouns are singular. Some (for example, *all, any, none,* and *some*) can be either singular or plural depending on the context of the sentence. Other indefinite pronouns (for example, *both, few, many,* and *several*) are *always* plural. The differences among these indefinite pronouns can be very confusing; determining what's right often requires an astute sense of proper English (or good memorization).

Compound Subjects. Most compound subjects (subjects joined by *and*) should be plural:

Kerry and Vanessa live in Nantucket.

The blue bike and the red wagon need repairs.

The reasoning behind this rule is fairly simple: You have multiple subjects, so you need a plural noun. Thus *Kerry and Vanessa **live**,* and *the bike and the red wagon **need**.*

PRONOUN-ANTECEDENT AGREEMENT

An *antecedent* is a word to which a pronoun refers later on in the sentence. In the sentence *Richard put on his shoes* for example, *Richard* is the antecedent to which *his* refers. When the pronoun does not agree in gender or number with its antecedent, there's an agreement error. For example:

Incorrect: Already late for the show, *Mary* couldn't find *their* keys.

Correct: Already late for the show, *Mary* couldn't find *her* keys.

Unless another sentence states that the keys belong to other people, the possessive pronoun should agree in gender and number with *Mary*. As far as we can tell, *Mary* is a singular, feminine noun, so the pronoun should be too.

The example of Mary contains a fairly obvious example of incorrect agreement, but sometimes the agreement error isn't as obvious. In everyday speech, we tend to say *someone lost **their** shoe* rather than *someone lost **his** shoe* or *someone lost **her** shoe* because we don't want to exclude either gender and because *someone lost **his or her** shoe* sounds cumbersome. You can argue in your spare time about whether *they* as a gender-free singular subject pronoun is acceptable, but remember that it's always wrong on the SAT.

Unclear Antecedents. You will also run into agreement errors in which the antecedent is unclear. In these cases, the pronoun is ambiguous. We use ambiguous pronouns all the time in everyday speech, but on the test (you guessed it) they're wrong.

> **Incorrect:** Trot told Ted that *he* should get the mauve pants from the sale rack.

This sentence is wrong because we don't know to whom *he* refers. Should Ted get the pants, or should Trot? You should restate the original sentence so that all the pertinent information is relayed without confusion or multiple meanings, such as *Trot told Ted that Ted should get the pants*.

NOUN-NUMBER AGREEMENT

Take a look at this sentence:

> All birds are very good at building their nest.

This may look okay, but it's incorrect. Do all birds share one nest? Nope, so *nest* should be *nests*.

Here's another common mistake the SAT will likely throw at you:

> Donna and Doug are planning to sell all their possessions and move to Maui in order to become a beach bum.

They are both moving, so *beach bum* should be *beach bums*.

Countability. Look at the following sentences:

I have *many failings*.

To mature is to transcend *much failure*.

Both sentences are correct. *Failings* is something one could count; *failings* are discrete entities like pebbles or atoms or four-leaf clovers. *Failure*, how-ever, cannot be counted; *failure* is an abstract state of being, like *sorrow*, *liberty*, and *happiness*.

Countability is most often tested via the *less/fewer* and *number/amount* pairings. After paying to register for the SAT, you have less money and fewer dollars. Sometimes the hardest writing question on the test simply requires you to notice that shift.

PRONOUN CASES

Pronoun case refers to the role of the pronoun in a sentence. There are three cases: nominative, objective, and possessive. You don't need to know the names of these cases, but you do need to know the differences between them. Here, we'll briefly describe each case.

The Nominative Case. The nominative case should be used when a pronoun is the subject of a sentence—for example, ***I*** *went to the store.* ***They*** *walked to the park*. You should also use a nominative pronoun after any form of *to be*:

Incorrect: It was *me* on the phone.

Correct: It was *I* on the phone.

The right sentence may sound awkward to you, but it's the correct use of the nominative.

In English, *to be* is a grammatical "equal sign," so when you have a sentence like *It was I on the phone*, you should be able to do this: *It = I*. If that equation holds true, *I* should be able to take the place of *It* in the sentence; thus *I was on the phone*.

The nominative also follows comparative clauses that usually involve *as* or *than*. When a pronoun is involved in a comparison, it must match the case of the other pronoun involved. For example:

Incorrect: I'm fatter than *her*, so I'll probably win this sumo wrestling match.

Correct: I'm fatter than *she,* so I'll probably win this sumo wrestling match.

In this sentence, *I* is being compared with *her*. Obviously, these two pronouns are in different cases, so one of them must be wrong. *I* and *she* are both nominative cases, so *she* is the correct answer.

Another way to approach comparisons is to realize that comparisons usually omit words. For example, it's grammatically correct to say *Alexis is stronger than Bill*, but that's an abbreviated version of what you're really saying. The long version is *Alexis is stronger than Bill is*. That last *is* is invisible in the abbreviated version, but you must remember that it's there. Now let's go back to the sumo sentence. As in our Alexis and Bill example, we don't see the word *is* in the comparison, but it's implied.

If you see a comparison using a pronoun and you're not sure if the pronoun is correct, add the implied *is*. In the incorrect sentence, adding *is* leaves us with *I'm fatter than her is.* That's just wrong, so we know that *she* is the correct pronoun in this case.

The Objective Case. As may be obvious from its name, the objective case should be used when the pronoun is the object of another part of speech, usually a preposition or a transitive verb (a verb that takes a direct object):

Preposition: She handed the presents *to them.*

Olivia made a cake *for* Emily, Sarah, and *me.*

Between whom did you sit?

Transitive Verb: Harry *gave me* the tickets.

Call me!

Did you *take him* to the movies?

In the second preposition example, two names appear between *for* and *me.* If this confuses you, eliminate *Emily, Sarah, and* to get *Olivia made a cake for **me.*** Then you'll see that *me* is the correct pronoun case, not *I* (as in *Olivia made a cake for I*). This strategy of crossing out intervening words also works in spotting the correct case for an object of a transitive verb.

In informal, spoken English, you will not hear *whom* used frequently, but in written English (particularly written SAT English), you must remember the all important *m.* As in the third preposition example, *between whom* is correct; *between who* is not. A good way to figure out if you should use *who* or *whom* in a sentence is to see whether the sentence would use *he* or *him* (or *they* or *them*) if it were rearranged a little. If the sentence takes *he* or *they*, you should use *who*; if it takes *him* or *them*, you should use *whom.*

The Possessive Case. You already know to use the possessive case when indicating possession of an object:

My car

Her dress

Its tail

Whose wheelbarrow

You should also use the possessive case before a gerund, a verb form that usually ends with *ing* and is used as a noun. For example:

When it comes to *my studying* for the test, "concentration" is my middle name.

Despite hours of practice, *her playing* is really terrible.

You can think of gerunds as verbs turned magically into nouns, so they need to be preceded by the same possessive pronouns that precede noun objects.

VERB TENSE

Verbs are the motors of language—literally, they're where the action is. Not surprising, lots of errors come from using the wrong verb tense.

VERB TENSE	INCORRECT	CORRECT
Present	Last year I live in Paris.	Currently, I live in Paris.
Past	Last year I will live in Paris.	Last year I lived in Paris.
Future	Next year I lived in Paris.	Next year I will live in Paris.

Now let's look at tense in a little more detail.

Past vs. Present Perfect. The *past tense* signifies that something has occurred or existed in the past. It is indicated by an *-ed* ending or an equivalent irregular form, such as *swam* or *sank*.

Helen *lived* in Troy long ago.

This means that Helen lived in Troy at some *definite* point in the past. She no longer lives there, for whatever reason.

The *present perfect tense* refers either to something that began in the past and continues into the present or to something that occurred in the past but still has some bearing on the present. It is indicated by using *has/have* plus the *-ed* (or the equivalent irregular) form of a verb:

Helen *has lived* in Troy before.

Unlike the previous sentence, this sentence means that Helen lived in Troy at some *unspecified* point in the past.

Helen *has lived* in Troy for twenty years.

This sentence means that Helen started living in Troy at some point in the past, never left, and is still living there in the present.

Past vs. Past Perfect. The *past perfect tense* (also known as "pluperfect") refers to something that began and ended *before* something else occurred in the past. The past perfect tense is "more past than the past." It is indicated by using *had* plus the *-ed* (or equivalent irregular) form:

Helen *had lived* in Sparta before she lived in Troy.

This means that Helen's presence in Sparta *preceded* her presence in Troy, which *itself* occurred in the past. As a rule, if there are two actions that occurred in the past, put the one that occurred deeper in the past in the past perfect tense. The more recent action should be in the past tense.

Essential Concept # 3: Sentence Structure

Other SAT Writing questions will test your knowledge of sentence structure:

- Active and Passive Voice
- Modifiers and Modification
- Clause Organization
- Sentence Fragments
- Comma Splices
- Comparisons and Parallelism

ACTIVE AND PASSIVE VOICE

The active voice usually requires far fewer words than does the passive voice to convey the same idea, and it's always correct on the SAT. In sentences that use the *active voice*, the subject does the action. For example, in the sentence *My dog ate a bunch of grass*, you immediately know who ate a bunch of grass—*the dog*.

The *passive voice*, in contrast, identifies the performer of the action later in the sentence, or even never. For example, the sentence *A bunch of grass was eaten* leaves the reader unsure of who or what did the eating. The passive voice creates weak, wordy sentences.

The following words will usually tip you off to the passive voice: *is*, *was*, *were*, *are* (or any other version of the verb *to be*), and *by*. If you see these words, ask yourself, What's the action and who's doing it? If the person (or entity) committing the action appears only at the end of the sentence, or doesn't appear at all, you're dealing with passive voice. Take a look at this example:

> After Timmy dropped his filthy socks in the hamper, the offensive garment was washed by his long-suffering father.
>
> (A) the offensive garment was washed by his long-suffering father
> (B) his long-suffering father washed the offensive garment
> (C) the washing of the offensive garment took place by his
>   long-suffering father
> (D) long-suffering, the offensive garment was washed by his father
> (E) he left the offensive garment for his long-suffering father who washed it

The underlined portion uses passive voice. The phrase *was washed* suggests that someone or something did the cleaning. The point is, you don't know how the socks got washed. In order to fix the passive voice, the performer of the action must get a place of prominence in the sentence and clear up what he or she is doing. In the example above, the correct answer must make clear that Timmy's father did the load of laundry. Both **B** and **E** fix the passive voice problem, but **E** is wordy and redundant, so **B** is the right answer.

MODIFIERS AND MODIFICATION

A *modifying phrase* is a phrase that explains or describes a word. In standard written English, modifiers usually appear right next to the word they explain or describe. When modifiers are placed far away from the word they describe, the sentence becomes confusing because it's often unclear which word the modifying phrase is referring to, as in the following sentence:

Eating six cheeseburgers, nausea overwhelmed Jane.

This sentence contains the dreaded *misplaced modifier*. We can logically infer that Jane was doing the eating, but because the modifying phrase (*Eating six cheeseburgers*) is so far from the word it's intended to modify (*Jane*), figuring out the meaning of the sentence takes a lot of work. It could very well seem as if *nausea* rather than *Jane* is being described. Therefore, the meaning of the sentence could be that *nausea* ate six cheeseburgers. The sentence as is does not convey the meaning the writer intended.

When you see a modifier followed by a comma, make sure the word that the modifier describes comes right after the comma. Here is a corrected version of the sentence:

After eating six cheeseburgers, Jane was overwhelmed with nausea.

The phrase *eating six cheeseburgers* describes what *Jane* is doing, so Jane's name should come right after the phrase. Now take a look at this sample question:

> Having a bargain price, Marcel snatched up the designer jeans right away.
>
> (A)   Having a bargain price, Marcel snatched up the designer jeans right away.
> (B)   Marcel who has a bargain price, snatched up the designer jeans.
> (C)   The jeans' bargain price led to Marcel's snatching them up.
> (D)   Marcel snatched up the designer jeans, due to their bargain price.
> (E)   Based on their bargain price, the jeans were snatched up right away by Marcel.

The misplaced modifier in this sentence confuses the meaning of sentence. As it is, it sounds like Marcel has a bargain price, but he certainly isn't for sale. That means you can cut **A** right away because it just preserves the underlined portion of the sentence. Cut **B** because it also identifies Marcel as the object with the bargain price. **C** uses the possessive awkwardly. **E** looks better, but the phrase *the jeans were snatched up* uses the passive voice (and the SAT prefers active voice—as stated in the previous section). **D** is the correct answer.

CLAUSE ORGANIZATION

A *clause* is a group of words that has a subject and a predicate. Sentences can have one or many clauses. You will see a good number of SAT questions that test clause organization. Here are some errors you could see:

The Weak **And.** *And* is pretty much the word version of the "+" symbol and denotes addition or the mere presence of two equivalent things at the same time or in the same place. Here's an example of *and* being used incorrectly:

> Bob Dylan's appearance in a lingerie commercial stunned many of his fans and much of his career had been devoted to debunking empty commercialism.

This sentence just cries out for causation. Substitute *because* for *and* to make this sentence correct:

Bob Dylan's appearance in a lingerie commercial stunned many of his fans *because* much of his career had been devoted to debunking empty commercialism.

That *vs*. Which. The SAT will test your understanding of restrictive and nonrestrictive clauses using *that* and *which*. Take a look at these examples:

The car that I have to repair is in the driveway.
The car, which I have to repair, is in the driveway.

The first sentence tells you which car is in the driveway: *that I have to repair* is a modifier of *the car*. It performs the same function that red or blue would if either were used as a modifying adjective.

The second sentence reports the repair of the car as incidental. *Which* is used, and the *which* clause is set off with commas. The sentence is a response to the question, *Where is the car?* If you see a *which* clause, remember that it's nonrestrictive—and make sure that commas set it off. Often the SAT will omit one of the commas.

SENTENCE FRAGMENTS

Sentence fragments are incomplete sentences that tend to look like this on the SAT:

We didn't go outside. *Even though the rain had stopped.*

Tommy could not pay for his lunch. *Having spent his last dollars on sunglasses.*

Always a bit shy. *She found herself unable to talk to the other kids.*

These sentence fragments are not sentences on their own. They can be connected to the independent clauses next to them to form complete sentences:

We didn't go outside, *even though the rain had stopped.*

Having spent his last dollars on sunglasses, Tommy could not pay for his lunch.

Always a bit shy, she found herself unable to talk to the other kids.

COMMA SPLICES

A comma splice occurs when two independent clauses are joined together by a comma with no intervening conjunction. For example:

Bowen walked to the *park, Leah* followed behind.

The comma between *park* and *Leah* forms a comma splice. Although the sentence may sound correct because the comma demands a short pause between the two related clauses, the structure is wrong in written English. There are three ways to fix a comma splice:

1. Use a semicolon.

Bowen walked to the *park; Leah* followed behind.

2. Separate the clauses into two sentences.

Bowen walked to the *park. Leah* followed behind.

3. Add a conjunction.

Bowen walked to the *park, while* Leah followed behind.
Bowen walked to the *park, and* Leah followed behind.

Inserting *while* subordinates the "Leah" clause to the "Bowen" clause. In the second sentence, the *and* joins the two clauses on equal footing.

COMPARISONS AND PARALLELISM

Check out this question:

> Like the Byzantines, who in the course of ruling the eastern Mediterranean basin for a thousand years left behind much-imitated traditions in law, art, and architecture, <u>Ottoman architecture often features huge domes</u>.
>
> (A) Ottoman architecture often features huge domes
> (B) Ottomans often features huge domes
> (C) Ottomans often built huge domes
> (D) huge domes were often featured by Ottoman architecture
> (E) Ottoman architecture often featured huge domes

It's illogical to compare *the Byzantines* to *Ottoman architecture*. You're comparing people to structures. Instead, compare like with like. The SAT makes things tricky by inserting a long intervening clause. To answer this question, ignore the clause that begins "who":

Like the Byzantines, Ottoman architecture often features huge domes.

No matter how long that intervening clause is, you still have to compare like with like; this sentence compares *the Byzantines* with *Ottoman architecture*. Given the choices, the correct answer is **C**, which compares Byzantines to Ottomans. **E** is the past tense of **A**, so that's no good. **B** is logically impossible because people can't feature domes, and **D** still compares Byzantines (people) to Ottoman architecture (objects). This kind of error comes up a lot in Improving Sentences and Paragraphs.

Like *vs*. As. Another key concept is the difference between *like* and *as*. Use *like* to compare nouns (persons, places, things, or ideas), and use *as* to compare verbs:

> **Incorrect:** That woman sings powerfully like Aretha Franklin once sang.

> **Correct:** That woman *sings* as powerfully as Aretha Franklin once *sang*.

Here is another version of the parallelism mistake you're likely to see:

> **Incorrect:** *Painting* with oils is easier than when you *paint* with watercolors.

> **Correct:** *Painting* with oils is easier than *painting* with watercolors.

Always make sure your verbs are in the same form.

ESSENTIAL STRATEGIES

You've already seen several examples of SAT Writing multiple-choice questions. Now it's time to see how to answer them, using three special step mehods (one for each of the three question types). We'll begin with Identifying Sentence Errors.

Identifying Sentence Errors Step Method

This question type only requires that you *recognize* a mistake—you don't have to fix it. Some questions will be correct; most will have an error in one of their underlined sections. No question will have more than one error.

Use the following step method every time you attempt an Identifying Sentence Errors question:

Step 1: Read the sentence and note the underlined words.

Step 2: Determine whether any of the underlined words are in error, in the context of the entire sentence, and eliminate those that are correct.

Step 3: If you don't find an error, E is correct.

Perform Step 3 only if you haven't identified an error in Step 2. Let's go through an example:

In <u>Victorian</u> England, hunger and unemployment <u>was</u> so prevalent that social
    A   B

revolution was a constant source of <u>anxiety for</u> members of the <u>upper class.</u>
                                      C   D

<u>No error</u>
  E

Step 1: Read the sentence and note the underlined words. Knowing the Essential Concepts will give you an advantage. If you have some sense of what to look for, you can predict the kinds of errors you're likely to see. Here, for example, if you know that the SAT loves to test verb tense and verb agreement, you might take an extra close look at **B**.

Step 2: Determine whether any of the underlined words are in error, *in the context of the entire sentence*, and eliminate those that are correct. Although an error may appear in an underlined portion of the sentence, in order to recognize the error, the function of that underlined portion must be considered as part of a whole. Don't judge the underlined portions in isolation from the sentence.

In Victorian England . . . sounds okay. Eliminate **A**. Anytime you see a verb underlined, check out whether it agrees with the subject. What's the subject here? *Hunger and unemployment.* A compound subject requires a plural verb. Choose **B**. We've found our error, so there's no need for Step 3.

Improving Sentences Step Method

Unlike Identifying Sentence Errors questions, Improving Sentences questions require that you not only recognize a mistake but also that you know how to fix it. Note that some Improving Sentences questions will have no error.

Use the following method every time you attempt an Improving Sentences question:

Step 1: Read the sentence and note the type of underlined word, phrase, or clause.

Step 2: Determine whether the underlined portion, in the context of the entire sentence, is in error. If not, choose A.

Step 3: If there is an error, generate a potential fix without looking at the answer choices.

Step 4: Compare your fix to the answer choices and eliminate any that don't match.

Step 5: Plug your answer back into the sentence as a check.

Let's see how the step method works by tackling an example:

Eager to pass his final exams, <u>studying was the student's top priority</u>.

(A)   studying was the student's top priority
(B)   the student made studying his top priority
(C)   the top priority of the student was studying
(D)   the student's top priority was studying
(E)   studying was the top priority for the student

Step 1: Read the sentence and note the type of underlined word, phrase, or clause. *Studying was the student's top priority* is a clause preceded by an introductory clause. Because the SAT just loves to test clause structure, you've isolated the likely category of error.

Step 2: Determine whether the underlined portion, *in the context of the entire sentence*, is in error. If not, choose A. Exactly who (or what) is *eager to pass his final exams*, the *student* or *studying*? We've got an error here! You can eliminate **A**.

Remember: If you're sure something is wrong with the underlined portion of the sentence, but you're not quite sure of what it is, just guess! The odds are in your favor even if you can only eliminate one choice.

Step 3: If there is an error, generate a potential fix without looking at the answer choices. Put *the student* next to the introductory clause: *Eager to pass **his** final exams, **the student's** top priority was studying.*

Step 4: Compare your fix to the answer choices and eliminate any that don't match. Now you can look at the answer choices:

(A)   studying was the student's top priority
(B)   the student made studying his top priority
(C)   the top priority of the student was studying
(D)   the student's top priority was studying
(E)   studying was the top priority for the student

The correct answer is **D**. **B** looks okay, but it's less concise than **D**. Sometimes you'll predict the precise answer; other times you won't. For some errors, the fix is almost predetermined; for others, more than one potential fix will do. The more clauses in the question, the more likely it will be that more than one fix could apply.

The correct answer cannot change the original meaning of the sentence. If you're stuck, eliminate any answer choices that change the original meaning in some way.

Step 5: Plug your answer back into the sentence as a check:

Eager to pass his final exams, *the student's top priority was studying.*

Improving Paragraphs Step Method

Improving Paragraph questions require you to read a series of paragraphs, determine their weaknesses, and then pick the answer choice that solves the problems best. On test day, you'll see one Improving Paragraphs passage followed by six questions.

The good news is that most of what we've said about Improving Sentences applies to their Improving Paragraphs cousins. One exception is that Improving Paragraphs questions do not always repeat underlined portions as **A**.

The questions that don't resemble Improving Sentences questions tend to ask about the main idea of the passage, or they provide topics or sentences not in the original passage that might be included and ask you whether or where you'd insert them.

Use the following method every time you attempt an Improving Paragraphs question:

Step 1: Read and outline the entire passage quickly.

Step 2: Read the question.

Step 3: Reread the context sentences.

Step 4: Make your own revision.

Step 5: Read every answer and pick the one that comes closest to your answer.

Now we'll see how the steps work by looking at a few sample questions.

(1) Japanese cuisine continues to grow in popularity in the United States. (2) Americans are already fond of Chinese food. (3) Now they are discovering that Japanese cuisine takes a similar set of basic ingredients and transforms them into something quite special. (4) That Japanese food is generally low in fat and calories, and offers many options for vegetarians and vegans, adds to its popularity.

(5) Americans' enjoyment of Japanese cooking is still largely limited to an occasional night out at a Japanese restaurant. (6) Actually, Japanese cooking is surprisingly simple. (7) Anyone with a standard set of cooking utensils and knowledge of basic cooking terms can easily follow the recipes in any Japanese cookbook.

(8) Since Japanese restaurants tend to be fairly expensive, one would think that fans of the cuisine would be excited about the possibility of making it at home. (9) Unfortunately, many traditional Japanese recipes call for costly ingredients that often can only be found at Asian grocery stores. (10) As these ingredients become more widely available at lower prices, we are sure to see a proportional increase in the number of people cooking Japanese food at home.

In context, what is the best way to revise and combine sentences 2 and 3 (reproduced below)?

Americans are already fond of Chinese food. Now they are discovering that Japanese cuisine takes a similar set of basic ingredients and transforms them into something quite special.

(A)   American people are already fond of Chinese food, and have discovered that Japanese cuisine takes a similar set of basic ingredients and transforms them into something quite special.

(B)   American people are already fond of Chinese food, and now discover that Japanese cuisine takes a similar set of basic ingredients and transforms them into something quite special.

(C)   Already fond of Chinese food, American people are now discovering that Japanese cuisine takes a similar set of basic ingredients and transforms them into something quite special.

(D)   Already fond of Chinese food, having discovered that Japanese cuisine takes a similar set of basic ingredients and transforms them into something quite special, American people like it.

(E)   American people are already fond of Chinese food; however, they are discovering that Japanese cuisine takes a similar set of basic ingredients and transforms them into something quite special.

Step 1: Read and outline the entire passage quickly. This first step never varies, and you only have to do it once per passage. When we say *quickly*, we mean *quickly*. It shouldn't take you more than 2 minutes to read the passage and write a quick sketch of what the paragraphs contain. As you read, sum up the purpose of each paragraph in a few words. Here's how we would outline the sample passage about Japanese food:

par. 1: food = popular.

par. 2: cooking = easy.

par. 3: ingredients can be $\$\$\$$, but getting cheaper

Notice how we used symbols and abbreviations. No one will see your scribbles, so write in whatever way is best for you. The outline should cover the key facts and purpose of the passage.

As you read the passage, you're going to see a lot of errors. Ignore them! Because the passage has more sentences than the questions can possibly cover, it's a waste of time to examine each sentence carefully. Your main goal in this step is to understand the purpose of the passage and to see how the paragraphs relate. The outline sketch you write as you read will make it easy to navigate back through the passage.

Step 2: Read the question. Don't look at the answer choices just yet. Our sample question asks you to revise and combine. We're dealing with connections within a paragraph (and between sentences).

Step 3: Reread the context sentences. *Context sentences* are the sentences before and after the sentence mentioned in the question. Your quick read-through of the passage will give you a general understanding of its subject. But to answer most Improving Paragraphs questions, you need to go back to the relevant part of the passage and reread it. Sometimes the context can help you spot errors and rewrite the sentences.

This particular question gives you an excerpt, but it's a good idea to go back to the passage and quickly check out the *entire* first paragraph. You won't be able to correctly answer the question unless you have an idea of how this paragraph works.

Step 4: **Make your own revision.** As on other types of multiple-choice questions, it's important to generate your own answer before hitting the answer choices. This way, you won't fall for tempting but incorrect traps.

You need a connection between the two sentences that links Americans' fondness for Chinese food to the rising popularity of Japanese cuisine. The author is stating that what happened to Chinese food is now happening to Japanese food: Americans already like Chinese food; now they're starting to like Japanese food more and more.

Try the following connection:

> Already fond of Chinese food, Americans are discovering that Japanese cuisine takes a similar set of basic ingredients and transforms them into something quite special.

We swapped *Americans are* with *already fond of Chinese food* in the first sentence and connected it with the second sentence by substituting *American people* for *they* in the second sentence. In the original, *they* refers to *Americans*, so we fused the sentences by substituting the pronoun's antecedent for the pronoun itself. Once those two changes are made, the rest of the sentence—*discovering that Japanese cuisine takes a similar set of basic ingredients and transforms them into something quite special*—follows unchanged.

Step 5: Read every answer and pick one that comes closest to your answer. Our choice is **C**. Note that these answer choices group:

    A, B, E *American people are . . .*

    C, D *Already fond of . . .*

If you had trouble coming up with a potential fix, or if you were pressed for time, let these groups guide you. At worst, you could eliminate some answer choices, guess, and move on.

As a check, plug your answer choice back into the original sentence or passage:

> *Japanese cuisine continues to grow in popularity in the United States.* **Already fond of Chinese food, American people are now discovering that Japanese cuisine takes a similar set of basic ingredients and transforms them into something quite special.** *That Japanese food is generally low in fat and calories, and offers many options for vegetarians and vegans, adds to its popularity.*

Here's another question:

> In context, what is the best word to add to the beginning of sentence 5?
>
> (A)   Yet,
> (B)   Moreover,
> (C)   Predictably,
> (D)   Fortunately,
> (E)   Undoubtedly,

We outlined the passage in Step 1. So we can jump straight to the next step.

Step 2: Read the question. You're adding a word to the beginning of a sentence, so a connection word is required.

Step 3: Reread the context sentences. By reading around the referenced sentence or sentences, you'll zero in on the local context in question and be in a good position to suggest a potential fix or answer.

In this case, you're asked to link the first word in the first sentence of the second paragraph to the first paragraph. You should reread the first paragraph as well as sentence 5.

Step 4: Make your own revision. The first paragraph states that Japanese cuisine is becoming increasingly popular. Then sentence 5 shifts the argument. Despite what has just been stated, there is an important qualifier: It turns out that this popularity is limited to restaurants; Japanese home cooking isn't catching on in the same way. This is the local context.

Some connection words that show contrast and fit this sentence are *however, yet, nevertheless*, and *still*.

Step 5: Read every answer and pick the one that comes closest to your answer. **A** works. **B** shows continuation, not contrast. At this point in the passage, there's nothing *predictable* about Japanese home cooking's relative lack of popularity at all, so **C** is out. Nor is there anything *fortunate* about it, from the author's point of view—quite the contrary—so **D** is incorrect. For **E**, consider whether such a claim can be made. It can't, so chop this choice.

Now it's time for the practice set.

PRACTICE SET

Now try out the following 15 practice questions using the step methods you just learned. Work through the guided explanations that follow to evaluate your performance.

1. If one <u>intends</u> to <u>excel in</u> a particular profession, <u>you</u> may <u>have to</u> invest
          A   B   C   D

    many years in specialized education. <u>No error</u>
                                        E

2. The cat is becoming <u>so popular</u> in <u>American homes</u> that <u>they</u> will <u>soon</u>
                             A   B   C   D

    overtake the dog as America's favorite pet. <u>No error</u>
                                        E

3. No matter how <u>conscientious</u> you brush your teeth, <u>you</u> should still
                   A   B

    <u>go</u> to a dentist for regular <u>cleanings</u>. <u>No error</u>
     C   D   E

4. The lightning bolt is such a <u>dramatic</u> symbol of power that <u>they are</u>
                                A   B

    often found <u>in</u> mythology in connection <u>with</u> ruling deities. <u>No error</u>
                C   D   E

5. <u>All</u> universities impose penalties <u>on</u> students who do not cite sources
     A   B

    <u>when</u> <u>he or she uses</u> other people's ideas. <u>No error</u>
      C   D   E

6. Because he was late to the <u>party was the reason the guest felt awkward when he was introduced to the host</u>.

    (A)   party was the reason the guest felt awkward when he was introduced to the host

    (B)   party; the guest felt awkward being introduced to the host

    (C)   party, the guest felt awkward when he was introduced to the host

    (D)   party, the guest was feeling awkward when to the host he was introduced

    (E)   party; and the guest was feeling awkward when he was introduced to the host

7. Having been an avid fan of music for most of her <u>life, the elderly woman found learning to play the piano very easy</u>.

    (A)   life, the elderly woman found learning to play the piano very easy

    (B)   life, learning to play the piano came very easily to the elderly woman

    (C)   life; the elderly woman was able to learn to play the piano very easily

    (D)   life, it was very easy for the elderly woman to learn to play the piano

    (E)   life, and the elderly women found learning to play the piano very easy

8. Jane Austen's novels are widely <u>read and they are studied every year</u> in universities throughout the world.

    (A)   read and they are studied every year

    (B)   read; they are studied every year

    (C)   read, every year they are studied

    (D)   read; and every year they are studied

    (E)   read and studied, every year

9. In addition to being highly regarded as a bandleader, <u>Duke Ellington is also admired as one of the world's finest jazz pianists</u>.

    (A) Duke Ellington is also admired as one of the world's finest jazz pianists
    (B) people also admire Duke Ellington as one of the world's finest jazz pianists
    (C) Duke Ellington was also one of the world's finest jazz pianists, and as such is admired
    (D) the world's finest jazz pianist; Duke Ellington, also is admired
    (E) Duke Ellington, also is admired as one of the world's finest pianists

10. The traveling circus made stops at small towns <u>that were all over the country during the last two years</u>.

    (A) that were all over the country during the last two years
    (B) throughout the country during the last two years
    (C) over the last two years that were all over the country
    (D) all over the country that were during the last two years
    (E) that were during the last two years all over the country

(**1**) Ludwig van Beethoven, one of the world's most famous composers, was born in Bonn in 1770. (**2**) Ludwig's father encouraged his son to play the piano, hoping that the boy would become a child prodigy. (**3**) Ludwig gave his first public performance when he was eight years old. (**4**) Employed as a musician in the Bonn court orchestra since 1787, Beethoven was granted a paid leave of absence in 1789 to travel to Vienna and study with Mozart. (**5**) He was compelled to return to Bonn so that he could look after his family after the death of his mother.

(**6**) In 1792, he moved back to Vienna and took lessons from Haydn and Salieri. (**7**) By 1795, he had earned a name for himself as a pianist of great fantasy and verve, and he was especially renowned for his originality. (**8**) Beethoven was also very interested in the development of the piano. (**9**) He worked with piano-building firms in Austria and England and helped in the development of the modern concert piano.

(**10**) Around 1798, Beethoven noticed that he was beginning to lose his hearing. (**11**) He withdrew from the public eye and limited his social contact to a few trusted friends. (**12**) People who understood his frustration and were patient with his disability. (**13**) The final years of his life were dominated by severe illness and by his responsibilities to his family. (**14**) He died in 1827, and some thirty thousand mourners and curious onlookers attended his funeral procession.

11. In context, what would be the best subject for a sentence to be inserted between sentences 3 and 4 (reproduced below)?

Ludwig gave his first public performance when he was eight years old. Employed as a musician in the Bonn court orchestra since 1787, Beethoven was granted a paid leave of absence in 1789 to travel to Vienna and study with Mozart.

(A) A list of Beethoven's most famous compositions

(B) A description of Beethoven's adolescent years

(C) A history of Beethoven's family

(D) An analysis of Beethoven's skill as a composer

(E) A question about Beethoven's motivations for moving to Vienna

12. In context, what would be the best word to insert at the beginning of sentence 5?

(A) Undoubtedly,

(B) Moreover,

(C) Unfortunately,

(D) Typically,

(E) Surprisingly,

13. Which of the following is the best revision of sentence 7 (reproduced below)?

By 1795, he had earned a name for himself as a pianist of great fantasy and verve, and he was especially renowned for his originality.

(A) By 1795, he had earned a name for himself as a pianist of great fantasy, verve, and, most of all, originality.

(B) By 1795, he has earned a name for himself as a pianist of great fantasy and verve, and he is especially renowned for his originality.

(C) By 1795, he had earned a name for himself as a pianist of great fantasy and verve. And, he was especially renowned for his originality.

(D) By 1795, he had earned a name for himself as a pianist of great fantasy and verve; and was especially renowned for his originality.

(E) By 1795, he had earned a name for himself as, most, of all a pianist of great fantasy, verve, and originality.

14. In context, what is the best way to deal with sentence 12 (reproduced below)?

People who understood his frustration and were patient with his disability.

(A) Insert "Such" before "people."

(B) Place it before sentence 11.

(C) Connect it to sentence 11 with a semicolon.

(D) Connect it to sentence 11 with a comma.

(E) Leave it as it is.

15. What description best fits the passage as a whole?

(A) An analysis of German music

(B) A piece written in praise of Beethoven's genius

(C) A study of the effects of illness on productivity

(D) A parody of Beethoven's character

(E) A short biographical history

Guided Explanations

1. C

The sentence opens with the word *one* as the subject. The second half of the sentence switches from *one* to *you* in **C**; this is the error you are looking for. The verb *intends* in **A** correctly agrees with its subject; *one* is third-person singular, and *intends* is the third-person singular conjugation of the verb *to intend*. The idiomatic phrase, *excel in*, **B**, is also without error. To *excel* in something means to be particularly good at something; the sentence makes the point that being particularly good at something requires many years of focused study. The idiom *have to* in **D** is also without error; the sentence demonstrates the necessity of studying for many years to become very good at *a particular profession*.

2. C

The sentence is trying to show just how popular *the cat is becoming*; the cat is *so popular*, **A**, that it will soon be more popular than the dog. The use of the phrase *so popular* is without error and sets up the rest of the sentence, where it will show to what degree cats have become popular. Where is the cat becoming so popular? In *American homes*, **B**. The word *American* is correctly put in is adjectival form to modify the noun *homes*. The pronoun *they*, **C**, refers back to the original subject of the sentence, which is *the cat*. Notice that whereas the word *cat* is singular, *they* is plural. **C** is the error here. **D**, *soon*, tells us when the author of the sentence expects the cat to overtake the dog in popularity; there is no error there.

3. A

The word *conscientious*, **A**, modifies *brush*, which is a verb. Remember, a verb must be modified by an adverb; however, the word *conscientious* is an adjective. **A** is therefore correct; *conscientious* should be *conscientously*.

The pronoun *you*, **B**, is used consistently as the subject throughout both halves of the sentence. The verb *go*, **C**, agrees with its subject, *you*, **B**. Finally, *cleanings*, **D**, is the noun form of the verb *to clean* and functions correctly as the object of the preposition *for*.

4. B

The adjective *dramatic*, **A**, correctly modifies *symbol*, which is a noun. The phrase *they are*, **B**, refers back to the original subject of the sentence, *bolt*. Note that *bolt* is singular; *they are* is plural. **B** is correct. The preposition *in*, **C**, is utilized correctly; it lets you know that the author is making his or her point according to the world of *mythology*. The preposition *with*, **D**, is an idiom used in conjunction with the word *connection* and is intended to clearly point out that *lightning bolts* are often associated with *ruling deities* in the world of *mythology*.

5. D

The sentence opens with the adjective *all* correctly modifying the noun *universities*. The idiomatic preposition *on* in **B** is also used correctly; an institution or an authority figure *imposes* a penalty *on* someone else. The word *when*, **C**, is also without error; it tells us under what conditions *all universities* place *penalties on* students. However, the phrase *he or she uses*, **D**, is problematic; it is supposed to refer back to the word *students*. Note that whereas the word *students* is plural, *he or she* are both singular pronouns; a pronoun must always agree in number with its subject. To be correct, *he or she uses* needs to be replaced by *they use*. **D**, therefore, contains the error in this sentence.

6. C

This sentence begins with the clause *because he was late to the party*. This is a dependent clause and needs to be followed by a complete sentence. However, the second half of the sentence reads *was the reason the guest felt awkward when he was introduced to the host*. This is not a complete sentence; you need to find some way to make the second half of the sentence complete. **B** and **E** attempt to fix the problem by merging both halves with a semicolon. But you can use a semicolon only if the sentence on either side is complete. **D** has a host of problems. The phrase *when to the host he was introduced* is awkward and wordy. A much better solution is **C**, which makes clear that *the guest was late to the party and felt awkward when he was introduced to the host*.

7. A

The phrase *having been an avid fan of music for most of her life* modifies the subject, *the elderly woman*. There are no problems here. In the second half of the sentence, you learn that the same elderly woman found *learning to play the piano very easy*. The subject and verb agree with each other, and the sentence as a whole conveys a complete thought. There are no errors, so the correct answer is **A**.

8. B

To combine the two independent clauses, you need to make one of the clauses dependent, using a conjunction like *and* or *but* and insert a comma, or use a semicolon. In this case, the two clauses are separated by the word *and*, but without a comma. **A** is therefore incorrect. Scanning the answer choices, you should see right away that choices **B** and **D** use semicolons. However, **D** uses a semicolon and retains the conjunction *and*. Remember, you can only use a semicolon to separate two complete sentences; **D** cannot be the correct answer. **B**, however, removes the conjunction *and*. Both halves of the sentence are complete; this is the correct answer. **C** removes *and* and puts in a comma; this creates a run-on sentence. **E** puts the comma after *studied*, but this merely makes the second half of the sentence, *every year in universities throughout the world*, incomplete and therefore incorrect.

9. A

Duke Ellington is the main subject of the sentence. The modifying phrase *in addition to being highly regarded as a bandleader* is immediately followed by the subject, Duke Ellington. This is the correct placement of both the modifier and the subject, leaving no confusion. A comma also correctly sets off the modifying phrase. The opening phrase *in addition to* signals that you are going to learn something else about Duke Ellington; in fact, he is *one of the world's finest jazz pianists*. There are no errors here, so **A** is the correct answer to the question.

10. B

The modifying clause *that were all over the country during the last two years* is intended to modify *small towns*. The wording is awkward and makes it sound as though small towns *were all over the country*—as though the small towns were moving around, which makes little logical sense. **C** makes things worse by separating the modifying clause *that were all over the country* from the word it modifies, *towns*. **E** causes similar problems by separating the verb *were* from *all over the country*. **D** confuses the words so much, the sentence is no longer complete. **B**, however, makes it clear that the small towns were *throughout the country*. This is the answer you are looking for.

11. B

What is missing is an account of Beethoven's life between the ages of eight and seventeen. In context, it would make sense for the passage to include a little bit about *Beethoven's adolescent years*, **B**. The passage does not list Beethoven's most famous compositions, **A**; chronologically speaking, Beethoven has not yet started to write his most famous pieces. *A history of Beethoven's family*, **C**, might make sense earlier in the paragraph but not between sentences 3 and 4. **D**, *an analysis of Beethoven's skill as a composer*, is also beyond the scope of the first paragraph, which tells you about the early part of Beethoven's life. Beethoven does not move to Vienna in the context of the passage until the end of sentence 4; it makes no sense to question his *motivations for moving to Vienna*, **E**, so early in the first paragraph.

12. C

In sentence 4, you learn that Beethoven was given money to leave Bonn to *study with Mozart*. In sentence 5, you are told that Beethoven was *compelled* to come home again to care for his family. You need a connecting word that highlights this reverse in behavior. **C**, *Unfortunately*, correctly captures the sense that Beethoven has changed his mind. We have no idea if this kind of behavior is *typical*, **D**, or *surprising*, **E**, for Beethoven, as nothing in the passage so far would indicate that either word makes sense. *Moreover*, **B**, does not express that Beethoven was *compelled* to return home. *Undoubtedly*, **A**, also does not address the unfortunate turn of events for Beethoven's education.

13. A

When items are listed in a sentence, they need to be placed in parallel form. Sentence 7 lists three items: *great fantasy, verve,* and *originality*. Notice, however, that the third item in the list, *originality*, is saddled with the clause *he was especially renowned*. The other two items in the list, *great fantasy* and *verve*, are not accompanied by this extraneous information. In order for this sentence to read correctly, you need to find a solution that will place all three items in the same form. **C** puts the third item in the list into a second sentence, but *and, he was especially renowned for his originality* is an incomplete sentence and causes a whole new set of problems. **D** attempts to separate the third item in the list from the rest of the sentence with a semi-colon, but this still does not put all the items in the list in parallel form. **E,** which might tempt you, ends with the list *great fantasy, verve, and original-ity*. However, notice that the earlier part of **E** contains this clumsy wording: *as, most, of all*. It is incorrect to separate the comparative phrase *most of all* by commas, making **E** grammatically incorrect. Only **A** solves the problem. The sentence in **A** ends as follows: *great fantasy, verve, and, most of all, orig-inality*. Now the three items—*fantasy, verve*, and *originality*—are all listed as nouns; in other words, they are listed in parallel form.

14. D

Notice that sentence 12 is a fragment; it does not express a complete thought. If you insert "Such" before "people," as in **A**, you would have the following: *Such people who understood his frustration and were patient with his disability.* This still does not make sentence 12 complete. Moving sentence 12 around, **B**, or leaving it as it is, **E**, also does not fix the inherent problem that sentence 12 is a fragment. You can only connect two sentences together with a semi-colon, **C**, if both sentences are complete sentences in the first place. Only **D** provides you with a grammatically correct way to deal with sentence 12.

15. E

The passage as a whole gives you a quick account of Beethoven, a formida-ble German composer. You need to find the answer that best restates this. **A** and **C** are beyond the scope of this passage. **B** and **D** may be tempting if you missed the tone of the passage. On the whole, there is very little to sug-gest that the author is really *praising* Beethoven, **B**, or making fun of him, **D**. Only **E** sums up the author's intention, which is to provide a *short bio-graphical history*.

INTENSIVE 3

Critical Reading Section:
Sentence Completions

Sentence Completions X-ray

Essential Concepts

Essential Strategies

Practice Set

SENTENCE COMPLETIONS (SCs) ARE ONE OF THE TWO question types found in the Critical Reading section. (We'll talk about the second type, Reading Passages, in Intensive 4.) You will encounter 19 SCs among the 67 Critical Reading questions.

SCs are exactly what they sound like. You're given a single sentence with a blank or two and asked to pick the word or words that correctly complete the sentence. The test makers use SCs to assess your ability to figure out how words relate to one another within the sentence. In short, SCs test your understanding of *vocabulary in context*. Now let's see what they look like.

On test day, remember to answer the easy questions before tackling hard questions. SCs appear in order of difficulty: The first third is easy, the second third moderately difficult, and the last third difficult.

SENTENCE COMPLETIONS X-RAY

Below is a typical SC with directions:

Directions for Sentence Completions: Each of the following sentences has had a word or phrase removed and replaced with a blank. Select the word or phrase that, when put back into sentence, produces the best possible sentence.

In the Middle Ages, when few women held true political power, the irrepressible Eleanor of Aquitaine ------- England while her son, Richard the Lionhearted, tramped through Europe and the Middle East on the First Crusade.

(A) domesticated   (B) ruled   (C) destroyed
(D) betrayed   (E) repressed

You're looking for the word that best completes the sentence. The key word here is *best*. You need to find the answer choice that is the best of all the possible choices, because every answer choice will make the sentence grammatically correct. There's only one right answer, however; the other four choices are wrong. These wrong answers may be anything from entirely nonsensical to insufficiently clear.

To find the correct choice, you'll use the context of the sentence to figure out what the missing word or words mean. Here, the answer is **B**. In contrast to other women of her time, Eleanor was in charge while her son roamed around Europe and the Middle East. Let's move on to the Essential Concepts now and further demystify the SCs.

ESSENTIAL CONCEPTS

Most Sentence Completions fall under one of three categories:

1. Continuation
2. Contrast
3. Amplification

There are typical patterns associated with each category, which we'll point out as we go. For now, we just want you to appreciate how knowing about these three typical SCs already gives your test performance a boost. Much as a shark will attack anything it perceives as "fishlike," you now have a "search image" that can focus your attack by helping you predict and recognize correct answers.

Essential Concept #1: Continuation

This simplest SC structure will *continue* the flow of the sentence, as this one does:

> The drummer's playing was so ------- that the other instruments couldn't be heard above the din.
>
> (A) quiet   (B) poor   (C) loud
>   (D) enthusiastic   (E) fast

If the drummer's playing drowned out the other instruments, then it must have been *loud*. **C** is the correct answer. **A** is the opposite of what's required. The other choices present other possible qualities of the drummer's playing, but none have anything to do with the other instruments' ability to be *heard*.

Here's a two-blank version of a *continuation* sentence:

> The drummer's playing was so ------- that the other instruments couldn't be ------- above the din.
>
> (A)   quiet . . played
> (B)   poor . . appreciated
> (C)   loud . . heard
> (D)   enthusiastic . . ignored
> (E)   fast . . discerned

Two-blank SCs tend to be harder because they contain more unknowns and usually require greater insight into sentence structure than is necessary for one-blank questions. Two-blank SCs, such as the previous example, often depend on vocabulary knowledge. If you don't know what *din* means, for example, this question will be a bit more challenging.

A doesn't make any sense—what would quiet drumming have to do with the ability to play the other instruments? And what would that have to do with *din*? Those who don't know what *din* means still have a shot at eliminating **A**. **B** is one of those nasty distractors that tempts those who grasp the SC's structure but don't know what *din* means. One could picture *poor* drumming ruining a listener's appreciation for the other instruments, but this sentence is about loudness. **D**'s first word fits the first part, but what does *enthusiastic* playing have to do with something the other instruments couldn't accomplish due to the *din*? Finally, **E** makes a leap from *fast* drumming to causing a *din*, which is not necessarily true. The drummer could be playing quickly *and* quietly. **C** is the best answer.

Essential Concept #2: Contrast

Another kind of SC will take you in one direction and then shift to the opposite direction. Here's a one-blank version of the *contrast* sentence:

Although the drummer played -------, the other instruments were clearly audible.

(A) quietly   (B) poorly   (C) loudly
    (D) enthusiastically   (E) quickly

Note how in contrast sentences you have to work backward. On its own, *Although the drummer played* ------- gives insufficient information. But the word *although* warns you that the drummer's playing will *contrast* with the effect you will see later on.

In the second part of the sentence, *the other instruments were clearly audible*, the last word gives you the vocabulary clue you need. *Audible* means "able to be heard," so how must the drummer have been playing to make the audibility of the other instruments surprising? What would complete the "twist"? **A** certainly won't—**A** is more of a continuation. Using *Although* wouldn't make sense if the drummer played quietly. **B**, **D**, and **E** provide potential descriptions of the drummer's playing, but none of them would have an impact on the other instruments' audibility, let alone in the surprising manner that would complete the "twist." So **C** is the answer here.

A two-blank version of this sentence could look like this:

Although the drummer played -------, the other instruments were clearly -------.

- (A) quietly . . missing
- (B) poorly . . ignored
- (C) loudly . . audible
- (D) enthusiastically . . unappreciated
- (E) quickly . . synchronized

Again, this one's tougher than the one-blank version in which *audible* was the critical piece that led to the correct choice. Here, it's missing from the SC, although *clearly* gives you a subtle clue. **A** creates an unclear sentence. What would quiet drumming have to do with the physical absence of the other instruments? In **B**, poor playing is associated with ignoring other instruments, which doesn't necessarily follow. **D** could work if *Although* were *Because*—that is, if this were a continuation, rather than a contrast, sentence. **E** is a little tricky because it encourages a rushed test taker to accept that the drummer's fast playing didn't throw off his fellow band members. But the actual meaning is a bit unclear. Were the other instruments clearly synchronized with each other? With the drummer? Both?

Remember, the instructions ask you to select the answer that *best* completes the sentence. **E** is clearly not the best completion of the sentence; **C** is. If you picked **B** or **E**, you probably made up a story to convince yourself or at least cause some doubt. But doing that never helps you on the SAT. Pick the straightforward approach and you'll get the point.

Continuation and Contrast Words. There are many words that stand for continuation; others stand for contrast. Here's a handy chart:

CONTINUATION	CONTRAST
also, and, as well as, because, since, therefore, thus	although, but, despite, even though, however, yet

These aren't all the words that could signal a continuation or a contrast, but if you see one of them, you'll know exactly what to do.

Essential Concept #3: Amplification

This kind of SC moves toward greater intensity. Let's look at a one-blank *amplification* sentence:

> At first merely -------, the drummer's playing rose to deafening levels as the concert progressed, drowning out all other instruments.
>
> (A) quiet   (B) poor   (C) loud
>   (D) enthusiastic   (E) fast

A is tempting because it's possible that the drummer started out playing quietly and later became *deafening*. But if that were the case, we wouldn't say *merely quiet*. *Merely* implies that the sound level was on the loud side to begin with, which is what **C** correctly provides. As in previous versions of this sentence, **B**, **D**, and **E** provide descriptions of drumming that have nothing to do with the sound level and don't necessarily relate. They each could be true, but *poor, enthusiastic*, and *fast* drumming aren't quite the same as *loud*.

A two-blank version of this example could take the following form:

At first merely ------, the drummer's playing rose to ------ levels as the concert progressed, drowning out all other instruments.

(A) quiet . . inaudible
(B) poor . . virtuosic
(C) loud . . deafening
(D) enthusiastic . . ecstatic
(E) fast . . rapid

We can see that something about the drummer's playing was amplified as the concert progressed. **A** presents an "amplified pair" but goes in the wrong direction: *Inaudible* means "quiet to the point of silence." We need something that gets louder, not quieter, as suggested by the phrase *the drummer's playing rose*. Also, the last phrase, *drowning out all other instruments*, lets you know that you need a pair of words that signify getting louder, which **C** provides. The words in **B** are opposites. Why would anyone use *merely* to describe a change from poor to virtuosic drumming (*virtuosic* means "expert")? If you picked **B**, think about your rationale for doing so: Don't pick an answer simply because it contains a difficult word. If one word is much more difficult than the others, it's likely to be wrong, but many people will pick it just because they don't know what it means.

D also provides an "amplified pair," as *ecstasy* is an extreme form of *enthusiasm*. But the last phrase requires a pair of words describing loudness, not enthusiasm. Finally, **E** provides two words that are at the same "level," so to speak. It's hard to figure out whether *fast* or *rapid* is faster. Also, speed is not necessarily the same thing as loudness.

Keep the three typical sentence types in mind as you read through the Forward and Backward Methods presented in the next section and as you work through the practice set:

- **Continuation** sentences show a cause-and-effect relationship between their parts.
- **Contrast** sentences contain a "twist." Something surprising occurs within the sentence.
- **Amplification** sentences present an idea or description that grows in magnitude—bigger, smaller, louder, quieter.

ESSENTIAL STRATEGIES

In this section, you'll learn two methods for solving SCs:

- **Forward Method,** which you should follow every time you attempt an SC
- **Backward Method,** which you should use when you can't successfully use the Forward Method; think of this method as your backup plan

The Forward Method

Here's the primary step method to use on SCs:

Step 1: Cover up the answer choices.

Step 2: Read the SC and determine its type.

Step 3: Supply your own words to complete the sentence.

Step 4: Match your prediction to the answer choices.

Step 5: Plug your choice back into the SC.

You should attempt these steps *every time* you attempt an SC. We'll show you how by working through an example. Later in this section, we'll review the Backward Method, which you'll use when stumped.

Ignoring criticisms that the film was excessively ------- and biased, the director resisted efforts to make changes designed to produce a less fierce, more ------- story.

(A)   placid . . prejudicial
(B)   tranquil . . neutral
(C)   brutal . . unfair
(D)   violent . . even-handed
(E)   long . . compact

Step 1: Cover up the answer choices. This step is pretty self-explanatory. You'll want to cover the choices so that you don't get influenced by them when you're determining the SC type (Step 2) or making your own answer predictions (Step 3).

Step 2: Read the SC and determine its type. Draw on your store of Essential Concepts to determine whether this SC is continuation, contrast, or amplification. The director ignored criticisms that the film was excessively *whatever it was*, specifically refusing to make changes that would have made the film both less than *whatever it was* and more than *the opposite of whatever it was*. Thus *whatever it was* has remained the same. Tough, huh? We've got a continuation SC. Armed with this information, you're better equipped to come up with your own answers in Step 3.

Step 3: Supply your own words to complete the sentence. You will see there is another class of context clues in this question. The units [------- *and biased*] and [*less fierce, more* -------] mirror each other. The first blank should match *fierce*; the second blank should match *biased*. Our predictions are *brutal* and *impartial*.

Step 4: Match your prediction to the answer choices. Armed with your proposed answers, you're now ready to look at the answer choices:

(A)   placid . . prejudicial
(B)   tranquil . . neutral
(C)   brutal . . unfair
(D)   violent . . even-handed
(E)   long . . compact

We need an answer for the first blank that matches *fierce* and an answer for the second blank that matches *biased*. Let's go through the answers one blank at a time: *placid* and *tranquil* don't work, so eliminate **A** and **B**. **C**, *brutal*, matches our prediction exactly, but **D**, *violent*, seems good too. Eliminate **E**, *long*.

Now we're down to two choices: **C** and **D**. Let's take a look at the second blanks to see what works: **C**, *unfair*, doesn't match our prediction, *impartial*. **D**, *even-handed*, does match, so it's the correct answer.

Step 5: Plug your choice back into the SC.

Ignoring criticisms that the film was excessively **violent** *and biased, the director resisted efforts to make changes designed to produce a less fierce, more* **even**-handed *story.*

Take the time to do this step! Accuracy is as important as speed, and choices can look very attractive until you've plugged them back in. Skip this step, and you risk a one-and-a-quarter-point turnaround: You'll not only lose the point you might have gained, but you'll also be docked a quarter point when you get the question wrong.

The Backward Method

As we stated earlier, you should try the Forward Method on every SC. However, if you're having trouble finding the right answer, try the Backward Method. It's particularly useful in these scenarios:

- **Scenario 1:** You can determine the SC type, but you can't come up with words to fill the blanks.
- **Scenario 2:** You've determined the SC type and have supplied words to fill the blanks, but you don't recognize the vocabulary in the answer choices.

To sum up: You should use the Backward Method when you can't successfully use the Forward Method; think of this method as your backup plan.

SCENARIO 1

If you can determine the SC type, but you can't come up with words to fill the blanks, here's what you should do:

Step 1: Use positive or negative signs to determine what type of word you will need.

Step 2: Assign positive or negative signs to each answer.

Step 3: Eliminate the choices that don't fit, then select from the rest.

Step 4: Plug your choice back into the SC.

Now let's tackle a practice question to see how the Backward Method works.

Some linguists argue that when the term "unique" is used loosely, the concept becomes -------, losing its power to identify people, things, or concepts that are one of a kind.

(A) conservative   (B) sensational   (C) domestic
    (D) scarce   (E) diluted

Step 1: Use positive or negative signs to determine what type of word you'll need. The concept clearly loses *power* when used too *loosely*, so you need a negative word of some kind.

Step 2: Assign positive or negative signs to each answer. Take a look at the answer choices and figure out which of these is negative, in the sense of "lessening." **A**, *conservative*, isn't a particularly negative word in this context. *Sensational* is too positive. *Domestic* is certainly not negative. It doesn't seem very positive, either—and words with neutral connotations can be used as a third category in the Backward Method. But we need a clearly negative word to complete this question. **D** and **E** are both negative, so let's go to Step 3 and see how this helps you when you consider the answer choices.

Step 3: Eliminate the choices that don't fit, then select from the rest. **A**, **B**, and C were too positive, so cut them. That leaves **D** and **E**. At this point, you've eliminated three options, so you're ahead of the game. You have a one-in-two shot at getting a point and a one-in-two shot of losing a quarter point. Those are good odds over several questions, so plug each choice into the sentence to see which "sounds" better, and choose that one.

A Note on Using Your Ear. Your "ear" is the way you use common sense to decipher language. Your ear's reliability depends on how much exposure to standard written English you've had. Nevertheless, we've all had some exposure and we know that slang is off limits on the SAT. So you can use your ear to hedge your bets.

In fact, "bet-hedging" is what the Backward Method is all about. Without this method, you have only a small chance (20 percent, actually) of getting a point when you're stuck. The wrong-answer penalty is designed to neutralize random guessing only. With the Backward Method, you raise your chances of getting a point by eliminating answer choices and guessing from what remains. Remember, you should guess whenever you can eliminate even one answer choice with a reasonable degree of confidence.

Step 4: Plug your choice back into the SC. The correct answer is **E**:

> Some linguists argue that when the term "unique" is used loosely, the concept becomes **diluted**, losing its power to identify people, things, or concepts that are one of a kind.

SCENARIO 2

If you've determined the SC type and have supplied words to fill the blanks, but you don't recognize the vocabulary in the answer choices, we've got a step method for you. But first, a warning: Don't automatically pick the hardest vocabulary word in the question. If there's one killer word you don't know, it's still probably wrong. Instead of simply picking the hardest word, use this strategy:

Step 1: Apply "deciphering techniques" to the vocabulary in the answer choices.

Step 2: Plug each choice into the SC.

Step 3: Plug your choice back into the SC.

Some SCs use very tough vocabulary in the answer choices. In fact, one-blank questions that appear later on in a section usually feature brutally difficult vocabulary. Let's take a look at one of those and use this step method to work through it.

The newly recognized amoral ------- of the natural world, which was traditionally seen as reflecting an ultimately benevolent purpose, was Darwin's most controversial intellectual legacy, generating strong reactions from those who wanted to preserve nature's supposed ratification of particular theories of eschatology.

(A) stochasticity   (B) malevolence   (C) determinism
   (D) progressiveness   (E) contingency

Step 1: Apply "deciphering techniques" to the vocabulary in the answer choices. Even if you figure out that this is a complex version of a continuation SC, and that you need a word that means "purposelessness," you still have to deal with those nasty answer choices. Here's where you can use "deciphering techniques."

A is a tough word, so let's move on to **B**, *malevolence*, for now. The prefix *mal-* means "bad"; the root *vol* means "will," as in the word *volition*. So *malevolence* should mean something like "ill will." The blank is actually contrasted with *purpose*, which is modified by *amoral*; **B** doesn't work here. Let's move on to **C**: You may not be familiar with *determinism* as a philosophical concept, but you might know what *determined* means in the sense of "ordained." That's actually the opposite of what you want, so cut **C**.

Progressiveness may be unfamiliar, but "progress" is certainly more familiar. Because *-ness* refers to a "state of being," a word that means "a state of being progressive" doesn't really work. As in **C**, this doesn't really match "purposelessness," so eliminate **D**. *Contingency* may stump you, but have you ever heard a form of this word in another context? Half-remembered phrases can help you. If you'd ever heard a sentence like, "getting this scholarship is contingent upon scoring in at least the 90th percentile on the SAT," then you'd have a shot at deciphering this word's meaning. It seems to mean that certain outcomes are not guaranteed but rather depend upon certain prior events: Score in the 90th percentile, get the scholarship. Does this match "purposelessness?" It just might—keep **E**.

Step 2: Plug each choice into the SC. Your job here is to "listen" for which choices sound best. Read both **A** and **E** into the SC and choose the one that best fits. You're down to a 50/50 chance to either gain a point or lose a quarter point, so you're well ahead of the wrong-answer penalty.

Step 3: Plug your choice back into the SC. As a final check, re-plug your choice into the SC. Here, **E** is correct:

> *The newly recognized amoral* **contingency** *of the natural world, which was traditionally seen as reflecting an ultimately benevolent purpose, was Darwin's most controversial intellectual legacy, generating strong reactions from those who wanted to preserve nature's supposed ratification of particular theories of eschatology.*

Contingency means "the state of being dependent on or conditioned by something else; not necessitated." *Stochasticity*, however, means "random or involving chance or probability," which is not exactly right in this context. After Darwin, nature was seen as neither progressive nor purposeful, but it was not seen as entirely random. *Eschatology*, incidentally, means "a branch of theology concerning the ultimate destiny of humankind or of the world."

PRACTICE SET

See how well you know SCs by trying your hand at those that follow. Don't forget to read the answers and explanations to all questions.

1. Despite harsh punishments for fugitive slaves and difficult journeys through the night, Harriet Tubman proved her strength in the years before the Civil War by ------- capture and ------- many slaves along the Underground Railroad.

    (A) avoiding . . barring
    (B) allowing . . advising
    (C) eluding . . guiding
    (D) disproving . . abandoning
    (E) choosing . . defending

2. Throughout the past decade, the turnip crop has been -------, sometimes yielding abundant harvests and sometimes offering only meager quantities.

    (A) unprecedented   (B) illusory   (C) temporary
        (D) unstable   (E) impracticable

3. As a painter, Raoul needs to improve his ------- skills; his palette is often striking, but his forms seem ill-placed on the canvas.

    (A) remedial   (B) compositional   (C) deductive
        (D) mnemonic   (E) intuitive

4. Although Rosa's apartment always seemed ------- to her guests, Rosa was not naturally ------- and had to make a great effort to keep her home in order.

    (A) harmonious . . congenial
    (B) nondescript . . understated
    (C) immaculate . . fastidious
    (D) impressive . . generous
    (E) respectable . . vivacious

5. The advent of the compact disc in the 1980s relegated the vinyl record album to -------, making vinyl more important as a collectible than as a means of distributing new music.

(A) perpetuity   (B) obsolescence   (C) success
(D) renown   (E) infamy

6. Last year, the president of the company donated ------- percentage of her income to charity, a shocking generosity unmatched among other executives of her stature.

(A) an incompatible   (B) a paltry   (C) a monolithic
(D) an exorbitant   (E) an unspoken

7. Driven by her competing desires to further her political vision and to pursue music, Joanna ------- her goals and became an activist folk singer.

(A) refuted   (B) combined   (C) disallowed
(D) gauged   (E) conceded

8. There was no need to send food supplies to the village after the devastating floods; the storehouses had been spared and the villagers had a ------- of grain.

(A) panoply   (B) regalia   (C) plethora
(D) bastion   (E) lacuna

9. The magnificent antique watch demonstrated both technical precision and aesthetic skill; the watchmaker obviously possessed a ------- talent.

(A) prodigious   (B) lamentable   (C) quotidian
(D) tenuous   (E) normative

10. As the year wore on, his study schedule, which was already -------, became so burdensome as to be completely -------.

(A) beguiling . . uncontrollable
(B) strenuous . . unmanageable
(C) unproductive . . discordant
(D) negligible . . purposeless
(E) impractical . . superlative

11. Not content to offer his readers a ------- account of his life in politics, Winston
Churchill ------- a deeply penetrating look at the inner workings of government.

(A) meaningless . . disavows
(B) facile . . provides
(C) hurried . . constructs
(D) precise . . promotes
(E) capricious . . unveils

12. The food critic called the new restaurant -------, going so far as to describe it as
-------; the menu, the service, and the décor had all been extraordinary.

(A) mediocre . . pedestrian
(B) preternatural . . déclassé
(C) glorious . . moribund
(D) irksome . . enervating
(E) astounding . . sublime

13. Nguyen prided himself on his -------, an understanding of others' feelings that
has earned him many friends.

(A) empathy   (B) temerity   (C) astuteness
   (D) lethargy   (E) sociability

14. The butcher, an especially ------- and devious man, often swindled his customers
by rigging the scales in his shop.

(A) furtive   (B) bellicose   (C) perceptive
   (D) emotive   (E) diligent

15. Though automobiles were relatively scarce in the first decades of the twentieth
century, by 1950 they had ------- to the point of -------.

(A) amalgamated . . invisibility
(B) aggrandized . . ambivalence
(C) proliferated . . ubiquity
(D) evolved . . fruition
(E) regressed . . dependability

Guided Explanations

We've labeled our explanations according to which method we used to answer the SC. On test day, remember to always try the Forward Method first.

1. C

Backward Method

If you didn't catch the logic of this continuation SC and weren't able to make a prediction based on it, you could still look at the word *capture* and ask yourself which word makes sense with it. Would *allowing, disproving,* or *choosing* work with *capture*? Not really. *Avoiding* and *eluding* both work, so keep **A** and **C**. Now check the second word of each choice against *many slaves along the Underground Railroad. Barring* doesn't work, but *guiding* does. It must be **C**.

2. D

Forward Method

You know the blank must be filled by something indicating that the turnip crop is *sometimes* one way and *sometimes* another. You can predict that the blank of this contrast SC will be filled with something meaning "unpredictable" or "changing."

Looking at the choices, *unprecedented* means "never seen before"; nix **A**. *Illusory* means "imaginary"; scratch **B**. *Temporary* means "not permanent." Is that the same as "changing" or "unpredictable"? Might be a close call, so hang on to **C**. *Unstable* means "tending to change." Is that a better fit than *temporary*? Yes, so keep **D** and eliminate **C**. *Impracticable* means "not capable of being done"; out with **E**.

3.   B
Forward Method

The main clause of this continuation SC, *Raoul needs to improve his -------
skills*, is followed by *his forms seem ill-placed on the canvas*. What you need
is a word that describes the ability to arrange forms.

Does *remedial* have anything to do with arranging forms? No; it means "supplying a remedy." Eliminate **A**. Does *compositional* have anything to do with
arranging forms? Yes; it means "having to do with composition," which is
the arranging of forms. Keep **B**. *Deductive* means "based on reasoning,"
mnemonic means "related to memory," and *intuitive* means "based on a gut
feeling." You can get rid of **C**, **D**, and **E**. **B** works and is correct.

4.   C
Backward Method

Reading the sentence, you can figure out that it has to do with "neatness"
because of *to keep her home in order*. So you should scan the choices and
eliminate anything that doesn't have to do with "neatness" or the lack
thereof. *Harmonious, nondescript*, and *impressive* don't have anything
to do with "neatness," so you should eliminate them. That leaves **C** and
E. Looking at *fastidious* and *vivacious*, you might not know the precise
definition of either one, but *vivacious* has *viv-* as a root, which means "life"
in Latin. Probably not related to "neatness." **C** is a better choice.

5. B
Forward Method

The main clause says that the status of the vinyl album changed in the 1980s (*relegated the vinyl record album to* -------) and that it stopped being used as *a means of distributing new music*. You need a word that relates to the process of going from used to unused.

Does *perpetuity* relate to the process? No; *perpetuity* means "eternity." Eliminate **A**. Does *obsolescence* relate to the process? Yes; *obsolescence* means "the state of being outdated." Keep **B**. What about *success, renown,* and *infamy*? None of them is related to the process of becoming unused, so eliminate all three. **B** is correct.

6. D
Forward Method

The main clause of the sentence tells you that *the president of the company donated* ------- *percentage of her income to charity*. The following modifier adds that it was *a shocking generosity*. The word *shocking* is what you're trying to match here. You can predict that the correct answer will mean "shocking."

Does *incompatible* mean "shocking"? No; eliminate **A**. How about *paltry*? No; eliminate **B**. What about *monolithic*? This one might be tough, so hang on to it for a second. *Exorbitant*? That might work as well, so hang on to **D**, too. *Unspoken* doesn't mean "shocking," so nix it. You're left with **C** and **D**. At this point you can use your ear and choose from the two for a 50/50 chance. Something *exorbitant* is "out of orbit" or, in modern terms, "out of this world." *Exorbitant* is a better choice. **D** is correct.

7.   **B**
Backward Method

If you weren't sure what the logic of the sentence required, you could focus on the main clause, *Joanna ------- her goals and became an activist folk singer.* Which word could work with *her goals*? Scanning the choices, *disallowed* seems unlikely; eliminate **C**. If you know the meanings of the other words, you can see that **B**, *combined*, is the best choice. If you don't know the meanings of *refuted, gauged,* and *conceded,* you could still see that *combined* would work and choose **B**. You could feel confident in doing so because if an answer choice clearly works, no other choice will also work. **B** is correct.

8.   **C**
Forward Method

The first part of the sentence lets you know that the village did not need extra food after the flood. The second part, containing the blank, explains that *the storehouses had been spared* and that the villagers still had grain. The blank, then, must mean something like "enough" or "more than enough."

Panoply means "a shining array"; eliminate **A**. *Regalia* means "the symbols of a rank, office, order, or society"; eliminate **B**. *Plethora* means "an excess"; keep **C**. *Bastion* means "stronghold"; eliminate **D**. *Lacuna* means "gap or empty space"; eliminate **E**. The only one that works is **C**: *There was no need to send food supplies to the village after the devastating floods; the storehouses had been spared and the villagers had a plethora of grain.* **C** is correct.

9. A

Forward Method

The second part of the sentence describes the watchmaker's talent. You know from the first part of the sentence that the watch was well crafted. So you're looking for a word that praises the watchmaker's ability. Something that says he *possessed* "an enormous" *talent*. You can predict the correct answer will mean "enormous."

Prodigious means "impressively large," so keep **A**. *Lamentable* means "regrettable," so eliminate **B**. *Quotidian* means "commonplace"; eliminate **C**. *Tenuous* means "having little substance"; eliminate **D**. *Normative* means "relating to a standard"; eliminate **E**. **A** is correct.

If you got stuck, at least you know you need a positive word, so you can try to eliminate the words you know are negative or neutral, such as *lamentable* (notice the root word *lament*, which means "to regret strongly") and *normative* (doesn't sound either positive or negative). You can guess from the remaining three.

10. B

Forward Method

The sentence sets up a comparison between the study schedule at the beginning of the year and at the end. By the end it had been amplified and was *so burdensome as to be completely -------*. You know that the second word must mean something close to *burdensome*.

Scanning the second word of each choice, *uncontrollable* in **A** and *unmanageable* in **B** stand out as possibilities. Keep them and eliminate the others. Now look at the first words of those two choices: *beguiling* and *strenuous*.

Which is a better fit? We know that the study schedule had become even more of a burden than it *already* was, so we need a word that suggests *burdensome* again. **B** is the better fit.

11. B
Forward Method

The contrast is between *deeply penetrating* and the blank in the modifier. You know the first word must be somewhat opposite to *deeply penetrating*, like "superficial."

Scanning the first words, *meaningless* and *facile* stand out as possibilities. Keep **A** and **B**. Eliminate the others. The second words in **A** and **B** are *disavows* and *provides*. *Disavows* means "to deny." Does that work in the sentence? Did Churchill deny *a deeply penetrating look . . .* ? No; eliminate **A**. **B** is correct.

12. E
Forward Method

The main clause states that the *critic called the new restaurant ----, going so far as to describe it as ----*. The second part of the sentence lets you know that the restaurant is top notch. So the critic must have called the restaurant "great" and gone so far as to describe it as "wonderful" or something like that.

Scanning the choices, the only words in the first column that mean "great" are *glorious* in **C** and *astounding* in **E**. The second word in **C** is *moribund*, which means "on death's doorstep." **C** doesn't seem likely. The second word in **E**, *sublime*, amplifies the meaning. **E** is correct.

13. A
Backward Method

The sentence makes clear that you're looking for something relating to the ability to keep and make friends. You might not be able to pinpoint exactly what nuance is required here, but you can get a general idea of the word needed. Scan the choices and keep anything that seems like it could possibly work. *Empathy* and *sociability* are definite keepers (for future reference, remember that the root *-path* means "feelings"; the word *pathetic* doesn't really mean "loser-ish" but rather "inspiring feeling in others, usually pity"), so keep **A** and **E**. You can be fairly sure it will be one of those two, because the test makers are not likely to give you too many choices that convey similar meanings; they don't want you to be able to argue with the way they choose to define terms. You can plug each one into the sentence and see which sounds better. Or you can guess for a 50/50 chance.

14. A
Forward Method

You know that the butcher is *especially* ------- *and devious* and that he *often swindled his customers*. So you need a word, like *devious* and *swindled*, that fits in with the idea of the butcher as "dishonest."

Scanning the choices, *furtive* means "secretive"; keep **A**. *Bellicose* means "warlike"; eliminate **B**. *Perceptive* means "insightful"; eliminate **C**. *Emotive* means "exhibiting emotion"; eliminate **D**. *Diligent* means "willing to put in effort"; eliminate **E**. Read **A** into the sentence: *The butcher, an especially furtive and devious man, often swindled his customers by rigging the scales in his shop.* **A** is correct.

15. C
Forward Method

When an item begins with *though*, chances are you're dealing with a contrast. In this item, the contrast is between the fact that autos were *relatively scarce in the first decades of the twentieth century* and the fact that *by 1950 they had ------- to the point of ----*. So you need two words that will convey the idea that cars became more common after 1950. The first blank is probably easier to handle and will probably mean something like "become more numerous."

Scanning the first words in the choices, *amalgamated* means "mixed," so eliminate **A**. *Aggrandized* means "made more important"; eliminate **B**. *Proliferated* means "increased in number"; keep **C**. *Evolved* means "developed gradually"; eliminate **D**. *Regressed* means "returned to a worse condition"; eliminate **E**. The second word in **C** is *ubiquity*, a tough word most people are not likely to know, but because only *proliferated* worked in the first blank, *ubiquity* must be correct for the second. Indeed it is. *Ubiquity* means "the state of being everywhere." That works in the context of this item. Read **C** into the sentence: *Though automobiles were relatively scarce in the first decades of the twentieth century, by 1950 they had proliferated to the point of ubiquity.* **C** is correct.

INTENSIVE 4

Critical Reading Section:
Reading Passages

Reading Passages X-ray
Essential Concepts
Essential Strategies
The Big 5 Question Types
Special Advice for Fiction
Practice Set

ON TEST DAY, YOU'LL SEE SEVERAL READING PASSAGES (RPS), followed by a total of 48 questions. There are three types of RPs on the SAT:

1. The *Long* RP, followed by up to 12 questions
2. The *Short* RP, followed by 2 questions
3. The *Paired* RP, followed by up to 13 questions

On test day, you'll see a mix of passage types, but the total umber of questions will always add up to 48. This Intensive will show you how to read these RPs and how to answer the questions that follow.

READING PASSAGES X-RAY

<u>Directions for Reading Passages</u>: Use the introductory material and the passage below to answer the questions that follow. Answer the questions based on the content of the passage.

The following passage is taken from an article on the architecture of the Etruscans, a tribe that dominated Italy before the rise of the Romans, and the Roman architect Vitruvius's On Architecture, *which was written in the first century B.C. during the reign of the emperor Augustus.*

Line   As we have seen, decades of archeological research have shown that Vitruvius's famous chapter on Etruscan temples idealized readily apparent diversity. Although Vitruvius did accurately capture the main features of the Etruscan style, actual Etruscan temples deviated quite significantly from his
5   ideal. We might ask why Vitruvius ignored the architectural diversity of the many different Etruscan temples with which he clearly was familiar. Answering this question provides some useful insight into not only Vitruvius's definition of

the Etruscan style but also the purpose of *On Architecture* as a whole.

Traditionally, scholars answered this question by pointing to Vitruvius's
allegiance to Greek philosophy. In chapter six, Vitruvius reports that he
has had the benefit of a liberal Greek education, which he recommends to
all aspiring architects. Without such broad training, Vitruvius argues, no
architect can understand proper architectural theory. For Vitruvius,
architectural theory rested on the principles of mathematical proportion
promulgated by such Greek philosophers as Pythagoras. These philosophers
believed that the universe was structured according to god-given mathematical
laws. They further believed that the harmonious mathematical structure of
the universe (the *macrocosm*) was reflected in the structure of the human
body (the *microcosm*). Vitruvius extended this reflection to architectural
forms. Temples, Vitruvius believed, must reflect the mathematical
proportionality of the body, just as the body reflects the mathematical
proportionality of the universe. Thus, Vitruvius claimed to "find"
correspondences between proportional measurements of the human body—
that the hand's length is one-tenth the body's height, for example—and
proportional measurements of the Etruscan temple. Vitruvius Hellenized
the Etruscan temple by superimposing Greek notions of mathematical
proportionality on his purportedly empirical description of the Etruscan
temple style.

Vitruvius's belief that specific natural proportions should be extended
to architectural forms does help to explain why he idealized Etruscan
temples. After all, mathematical models generally don't allow for much
deviation. However, far more mundane considerations acted in concert
with Vitruvius's allegiance to Greek notions of mathematical harmony to
encourage the idealization of the Etruscan temple.

Despite its title, *On Architecture* was not written primarily for architects.
It was written to convince the emperor Augustus, the most powerful patron
in Rome, to give Vitruvius the opportunity to do large-scale architectural
work. Vitruvius knew that if Augustus devoted any time at all to *On
Architecture*, the emperor would most likely do what busy executives still
do to this day: He would read the introductions to each of the ten chapters
and skip the rest of the book. Reading *On Architecture* in this manner—
each introduction in sequence—is a revelation. One quickly realizes that
the chapter introductions constitute an ancient résumé designed to convince
Augustus to entrust part of his architectural legacy to Vitruvius.

Moreover, one must also keep in mind that *On Architecture*, like all
ancient books, was originally published as a series of scrolls. Each modern
"chapter" most likely corresponds to one ancient scroll. This physical form

lent even greater significance to the snappy, pertinent introductions and the concise writing that modern readers also demand. The physical act of
50 reading a scroll made the kind of flipping back and forth that modern paginated books allow significantly more inconvenient. Scrolls strongly encouraged ancient authors to front-load the most important ideas they wanted to convey. The ancient author had to earn each "unrolling" by concentrating that much more on the order in which ideas were presented
55 and the economy with which they were expressed—and how much more so when one's intended audience is the emperor of Rome?

Vitruvius's idealization of Etruscan temples now becomes even more understandable. Tellingly, Vitruvius buried his discussion of Etruscan temples toward the end of a chapter (i.e., scroll), which reveals that
60 Vitruvius considered Etruscan temples to be relatively unimportant. In the unlikely event that Augustus (or his appointed reader) might have actually put in the effort to reach this discussion, the last thing Vitruvius would have wanted his exalted audience to encounter is any unnecessary detail. In order to capture Augustus' attention—and patronage—Vitruvius had to
65 demonstrate his complete command of architecture in the smallest, most easily digestible package possible. The purpose of *On Architecture* was not to record architectural variety in encyclopedic detail but rather to gain architectural commissions. This fact, along with Vitruvius's fundamental belief in proportionality, goes a long way toward explaining why Vitruvius
70 ignored the architectural diversity he doubtless saw in Etruscan temples.

As used in line 11, the word "liberal" most nearly means

(A) tolerant
(B) generous
(C) free-thinking
(D) wide-ranging
(E) narrow

On the whole, the author's attitude toward the traditional scholarly explanation of Vitruvius's description of the Etruscan temple style described in lines 12–34 is one of

(A) indifference
(B) respect
(C) frustration
(D) interest
(E) mistrust

The principal function of the fifth paragraph (lines 45–56) is to show

(A) that contemporary architects did not find *On Architecture* helpful to their work
(B) why Vitruvius ended up building so many structures for Augustus
(C) how Vitruvius constructed *On Architecture's* ten chapters with his audience's likely reading habits in mind
(D) that Augustus was as busy as any modern-day executive
(E) how the nature of ancient scrolls discouraged readers

The author would most likely agree that the physical form of ancient books

(A) prevented ancient authors from writing as well as modern authors
(B) encouraged the writing of encyclopedic overviews
(C) was responsible for the spread of ancient knowledge
(D) is a unique source of insight into ancient writing largely ignored by traditional scholars
(E) undermined the ability of ancient authors to gain patrons

The main purpose of the passage is to

(A) expose Vitruvius's dishonesty
(B) prove the value of a Greek education
(C) suggest that Vitruvius considered Etruscan temples to be the most important type of temple
(D) discuss the differences between ancient scrolls and modern books
(E) account for the difference between Vitruvius's written description of Etruscan temples and their archaeological remains

The directions tell you to answer the questions based on the passage—not on outside knowledge. So even if you're an expert in Roman architecture, you'd still want to read the passage—and base the answers to the questions on what you'd just read.

The questions following the passage are not ordered by difficulty. Instead, RP questions are ordered by what part of the passage they refer to. Questions that test the beginning of the passage appear at the beginning of the group, questions that test the middle appear in the middle, and questions that cover the end appear at the end. General questions that cover the entire passage may appear at the beginning or the end—but not the middle. Passages, on the other hand, do tend to get harder as the section goes on.

The Long RP

As you can see from the X-ray, a Long RP consists of directions, an italicized introduction, and several paragraphs followed by several questions. (On test day, the Long RPs you see may be followed by up to twelve questions.) Each question has five answer choices. One of these answer choices is correct; the other four answer choices are not. Line numbers are given in the left-hand margin, as shown. We'll go over how to answer these questions in the section on the Big 5 Question Types.

The Short RP

Short RPs are one or two paragraphs long and around 100 to 200 words total. Each Short RP is followed by between two and five questions. Short RPs and questions are really just scaled-down Long RPs and questions (which is part of the reason we're using a Long RP to introduce you to the Essential Concepts). There's nothing particularly unique about Short RPs. If anything, the language in the passage seems to be a little easier to understand than that of a Long RP.

The Paired RP

Paired RPs consist of two passages and several questions. Both passages discuss the same topic or theme, but each one takes a different position on the subject matter. The first few questions are based on Passage 1, the next few questions are based on Passage 2, and the last few questions are based on both passages. Each passage is around 250 to 600 words long, a little longer than a Short RP and a little shorter than a Long RP. You will see at least one Paired RP on test day. You may see Paired *Short* RPs as well, which contain fewer paragraphs and questions.

Passage Types

Passages can be either nonfiction or fiction. Nonfiction passages can be on any topic in one of three broad areas: science, social science, and the humanities. Questions are never based on outside knowledge; all the information you need to answer the questions is in the passage. Passages may feature a couple of unfamiliar terms related to the topic at hand, but these terms are always defined within the passage.

Fiction RPs will be straightforward, conventional, and most likely concerned with issues of personal development or family relationships. The SAT tends to stay away from controversial topics such as war, sex, death, religion, or politics. Although some familiarity with basic literary techniques is required, the fiction RPs are pretty similar to the nonfiction RPs. If you've taken an English class recently, you probably already know the literary techniques, but we'll review them a little later in this Intensive.

ESSENTIAL CONCEPTS

Long, Short, and Paired RP questions all measure how well you've understood the passage you've just read. So, to answer these questions correctly, you need to be able to read the passages quickly and accurately. Our Essential Concepts will teach you to do just that. Before you tackle RPs and their questions, you need to be familiar with the major features of an RP:

1. Topic and Scope
2. Purpose and Main Idea
3. Tone

Essential Concept #1: Topic and Scope

The *topic* is the subject matter treated in a passage. The *scope* is the breadth of the topic covered in the passage. In our sample passage, the topic is Vitruvius's book about architecture. The questions will test whether you picked up on the *specific aspect* of Vitruvius's book that the passage covers. On your own, come up with your definition of this passage's scope, then look at our chart to see how your answer matches up.

EXAMPLE OF TOPIC'S SCOPE	DESCRIPTION OF SCOPE
Architecture	way, way too broad
The history of Roman architecture	way too broad
Descriptions of Etruscan temples	too broad
Reasons why Vitruvius ignored diversity in Etruscan temples	just right
Vitruvius's understanding of Greek philosophy	too narrow
The importance of natural proportions to architecture	way too narrow
The abilities of Augustus as a ruler	off topic

One way to think of scope is to compare it to the frame of a photograph. If you want to photograph, say, your house, you'll certainly want something between a satellite photo of the entire Earth (too broad) and an electron micrograph of the wood on your front door (too narrow). And you don't want a picture of someone else's house or of, say, the White House or the Empire State Building ("off topic"). You'll want just the front of the house with a little space on all sides to show a bit of the yard and trees.

Lots of SAT questions require you to know what the passage covers and what it doesn't. Other questions require you to identify the author's focus or concerns—anything outside the scope of the passage can't be a focus or concern of the author. Understanding topic and scope will also help you when you get to the answer choices: Answers that are "out in left field"—i.e., outside the scope—are almost always wrong.

Essential Concept #2:
Purpose and Main Idea

The *purpose* of the passage is the reason the author is writing. Every passage has a purpose, and authors write to express a specific main idea. The *main idea* of a passage is the central point that the author is making. It is a clear expression of the topic and scope, along with the author's particular take on that topic and scope.

In our sample passage, the author comes right out and states her purpose in the first paragraph: She wants to figure out *why* Vitruvius disregarded the many different types of Etruscan temples.

Frequently, RP questions will combine these main idea questions with purpose questions; for example, you might be asked to identify the main purpose of an RP, as in our final sample question. The main idea is also helpful in other kinds of questions. For example, if you're asked for a statement with which the author will agree, the correct answer will be consistent with the purpose of the passage. Wrong answers often conflict with the author's purpose or the main idea. Even for those questions that are not explicitly "global," knowing the purpose/main idea can help you eliminate distractors.

Essential Concept #3: Tone

Tone is based both on a passage's style and on the particular words used in the passage. The way an author uses language indicates the author's attitude toward his or her subject matter. Tone may be subjective, objective, positive, negative, neutral, or one of a whole range of adjectives.

In the Vitruvius passage, the author's tone is respectfully academic. She discusses the facts objectively.

Like purpose and main idea, tone is often tested directly. Knowing the author's tone helps you answer other questions, such as questions about the author's point of view about a particular aspect of the topic. Remember too that correct answers to *all* questions tend to agree with the author's tone. Incorrect answers conflict with the author's tone.

ESSENTIAL STRATEGIES

In this section, we explain what to do to each and every SAT RP:

- Skim
- Identify Essential Concepts
- Outline
- Make a Prediction
- Eliminate Extreme Answers
- Use the RP Step Methods

Let's see how these techniques work.

Skim

Because of the time constraints, SAT reading is not like normal, everyday reading. Normal, everyday reading means reading every single word of a passage at least once. *Skimming* means reading only some of the words in a passage and letting your eyes dart across the rest.

The key to skimming is breaking the habit of reading a passage word for word. This is an essential skill for succeeding on RPs because it leads to significant time savings.

Here's how you do it: Use a pencil or pen to help you break the habit of reading every word. Move the tip of your pencil across the lines of text quickly enough to make it impossible for you to read every word. This forces you to skip over some words and phrases, which means you are actually *skimming*. Circle or underline signpost words or key terms. The idea is to identify some important terms, as well as those important signpost words.

Always skim Long RPs and Paired RPs. Short RPs are too short to skim. Go ahead and read every word.

Identify Essential Concepts

As you read, think about the passage's topic and scope, purpose and main idea, and tone. You might even jot these down in the margins of your test booklet so that they stay utmost in your mind.

Here are our notes on the Essential Concepts of the Vitruvius passage:

Topic & Scope	V's book on architecture/Reasons why V ignored diversity in Etruscan temples
Purpose	To introduce another explanation for why V ignored diversity in Etruscan temples
Main Idea	Along with traditional interpretation—V. liked Greek phil.—author adds that purpose of book (to get work for V.) and scroll-nature of book explain lack of diversity.
Tone	Respectfully academic; a discussion

Your notes about "the big picture" will help you answer the general questions dealing with main points, point of view, and tone easily.

Outline

In addition to your notes about the Essential Concepts, you should also mark up the passage, underlining key phrases and making notes about each paragraph. Later you can use your underlines and notes as a map through the passage, so that you don't waste time covering passage territory for a second time.

Underline the topic sentence of each paragraph; doing so will help you keep on top of the argument's direction. Write "ex" or "x" where the author gives examples that support his or her argument. You might also use checkmarks or asterisks to note key phrases or ideas. Do whatever works for you as long as your scribbles, doodles, and underlines form an outline that lets you quickly identify the passage's important points. Don't try to provide a complete reference guide to the passage. Your outline is meant to prevent you from getting distracted and to give you a quick summary of the passage's key points.

Here's our version of the margin notes/outline:

First "quarter": the italicized intro, Paragraph 1, and part of Paragraph 2	Vitr. and Etruscan temples—why no diversity—why did he simplify in his book? 1st reason: traditional; Greek proportionality
Paragraph 3	Another reason—more mundane
Paragraph 4	O.A. not for archs—it's V.'s résumé
Paragraph 5	O.A. originally scrolls, not book
Paragraph 6	Résumé + scrolls = another reason for lack of diversity in Et. temples

Make a Prediction

This strategy applies to many SAT questions. Making a prediction about the answer as you read the question reduces the likelihood that you'll fall for traps. But it's particularly helpful on RPs because the questions are often long and wordy, which can make this section quite challenging. If you can formulate your own answer, you'll stay focused and not get caught up in answer choices that are there to distract you.

So before going back to the passage, articulate to yourself exactly what the question is asking. Don't look at the answers. Instead, try to formulate an answer in your own words. Then quickly scan the answer choices and choose the one that best matches your version.

Eliminate Extreme Answers

We want to say a few more things about the answer choices you'll see before we talk about the step methods you should use. In fact, we want to point out a key feature of the answer choices: Choices with "extreme" language are usually wrong, regardless of the question type. So if you can't find an answer that matches your prediction, you should eliminate extreme answers and guess from the remaining choices.

Look at the following chart:

TIME	SPACE OR AMOUNT
Never	None
Rarely	A little/few
Sometimes	Some
Often/frequently	A lot/most
Always	All

The extreme terms are at the top and bottom of this chart; the middle terms are more measured, and therefore more likely to be correct when applied to any statement.

Another term to watch out for is *only*. This doesn't quite fit into the chart above, but it nevertheless has a very restrictive meaning—and it's "extreme" in the sense we're discussing now. For example, the statement "The Beatles were the only worthwhile rock group that was active in the 1960s" is pretty extreme. All you would need to do to refute that statement is present a halfway-decent argument that any other 1960s rock group was "worthwhile." Beware of the word *only*.

Use the RP Step Methods

We have provided a step method for each of the three types of RPs. We'll begin with the Long RP.

THE LONG RP STEP METHOD

Here are the steps you should follow on Long RPs and their questions:

Step 1: Skim and outline the passage.

Step 2: Answer specific questions.

Step 3: Answer general questions.

Now let's discuss them in more detail.

Step 1: Skim and outline the passage. Concentrate on the introduction, conclusion, the first main paragraph, and the first and last sentences of every subsequent paragraph. Don't forget to take notes! Again, your outline and notes should be similar to the ones we took on the Vitruvius passage earlier in this Intensive.

Step 2: Answer specific questions. Specific questions refer directly to words or lines in the passage. Before going back to the paragraph, articulate to yourself exactly what the question is asking. When you're clear on the question, go to the specific area in the passage and read just the few lines above and below it to get a sense of the context. Come up with your own answer to the question *first, then* find the answer choice that matches yours. We explain more about specific questions in the section on the Big 5 Question Types later in this Intensive.

Step 3: Answer general questions. General questions ask about broad aspects of the passage, such as its main idea, tone, and argument. You should be able to answer them without looking back at the passage; instead, use your notes and outline to answer general questions. We explain more about general questions in the section on the Big 5 Question Types later in this Intensive.

THE SHORT RP STEP METHOD

And here are the steps you should follow on Short RPs and their questions:

Step 1: Read the questions but not the answer choices.

Step 2: Read the passage, with special focus on answering the questions.

Step 3: Come up with answers for the questions in your own words.

Step 4: Match your answers to the correct answers.

The Practice Set at the end of this Intensive has a Short RP and a few questions, so you'll know what to expect on test day. Here's how the steps work:

Step 1: Read the questions but not the answer choices. For Long RPs, we advised you to skim and outline the entire passage, *then* check out the questions that follow. But Short RPs are short enough that you can comfortably fit the entire passage and questions in your head. Skipping the answer choices means you won't be distracted by potential pitfalls.

Step 2: Read the passage, with special focus on answering the questions. Short RPs don't require an outline, but you should still circle or underline key words and phrases. If you read the questions beforehand, you'll know exactly what to look for as you read the passages.

Step 3: Come up with answers for the questions in your own words. Predicting the answers to questions will help you to avoid distractors and traps.

Step 4: Match your answers to the correct answers. Scan the answer choices and pick the one that best resembles your prediction. If you get stuck, you can quickly re-read the Short RP without losing too much time.

THE PAIRED RP STEP METHOD

Paired RPs require a slightly different strategy. The SAT organizes Paired RP questions as follows:

- Questions concerned with the first passage come first.
- Questions concerned with the second passage come next.
- The final few questions will deal with both passages, usually asking you to compare and contrast.

Here's the step method to use on Paired RPs:

Step 1: Read the introduction, then the first passage.

Step 2: Answer the questions about the *first passage only*.

Step 3: Read the second passage.

Step 4: Answer the questions about the *second passage only*.

Step 5: Answer the remaining questions.

Below we explain how the Paired RP step method works. For more practice, turn to the Practice Set at the end of this Intensive.

Step 1: Read the introduction, then the first passage. The italicized introduction gives you valuable info about the passages that follow. It's your first clue to the topic, scope, purpose, and main idea. After the intro, quickly skim and outline the first passage. Treat the first passage like a Long RP.

Step 2: Answer the questions about the *first passage only*. Hit the questions about the first passage first, while the passage's content is still fresh in your mind. Basically, ignore the second passage for the time being. The questions will be ordered such that the first few deal with the first passage, the second few questions deal with the second passage, and the final questions deal with both passages together.

Step 3: Read the second passage. Once you've answered the first passage's questions, turn your attention to the second passage. Again, treat this passage like a Long RP by skimming, noting its major features, and jotting down an outline.

Step 4: Answer the questions about the *second passage only*. Resist the temptation to answer all the questions. Just focus on the questions that deal with the second passage.

Step 5: Answer the remaining questions. By the time you've dealt with the two passages individually, you'll have built up a strong enough understanding to be able to answer the remaining questions, which ask you to *relate* the two passages. These "relating" questions usually ask you to compare a variety of aspects of the two RPs, such as the main ideas, arguments, and tones. Sometimes these questions get a bit more creative and ask you to predict or infer something about how author 1 would feel about something author 2 says or vice versa.

THE BIG 5 QUESTION TYPES

Regardless of their length, RPs always test the skills needed to make sense of paragraphs and longer chunks of prose. Keep this in mind as we cover the five major question types, which we've ordered from most specific to most general. You'll see these questions after Long, Short, and Paired RPs.

QUESTION TYPE	YOUR TASK
1. Vocabulary in Context	Understand the meaning of a word in relation to the sentence or passage
2. Literal Comprehension	Demonstrate your understanding of specific aspects of the passage
3. Attitude	Identify the writer's attitude toward the subject
4. Big Picture/Purpose	Identify the passage's purpose or main idea
5. Inference	Take something given in the passage and use it to figure out something else

As we mentioned earlier, the questions following the passages are ordered by what part of the passage they refer to. The key with all RP questions is to have some idea of the answer *before* you look at the answer choices. Putting the answer into your own words will help you avoid distractors.

Let's go over how to answer each type of question. Along the way, we'll also explain which types are specific (and therefore should be answered in

Step 2 of the Long RP step method) and which types are general (and therefore should be answered in Step 3 of the Long RP step method). All our sample questions refer to the Vitruvius passage in the X-ray.

1. Vocabulary in Context

As used in line 11, the word "liberal" most nearly means

(A) tolerant
(B) generous
(C) free-thinking
(D) wide-ranging
(E) narrow

Always answer Vocabulary-in-Context (VIC) questions first because they refer to specific parts of the RP. In this question type, you're usually directed back to the passage, so you should re-read the referenced lines. The key to VICs is going back to the sentence that's referenced, as well as the sentences before and after.

Traditionally, scholars answered this question by pointing to Vitruvius's allegiance to Greek philosophy. In chapter six, Vitruvius reports that he has had the benefit of a **liberal** *Greek education, which he recommends to all aspiring architects. Without such broad training, Vitruvius argues, no architect can understand proper architectural theory.*

The main idea of this chunk is that traditional scholars attributed Vitruvius's treatment of Etruscan temples to his adherence to Greek philosophical ideas of proportionality.

Try taking out the word *liberal* and seeing what else would work grammatically. Notice that the phrase *without such broad training* gives you a clue as to what the "missing" word should be. Note that *liberal* is one of those words that has several common meanings. Naturally, these are the kinds of words that usually show up in VICs. This question type tests not just vocabulary, but vocabulary *in context*.

You always want to generate a potential answer *without* looking at the answer choices. We're looking for something like *broad*. Don't fret too much about coming up with the perfect prediction. A phrase will do just fine because the correct answer is often a phrase, rather than a specific word.

Compare your potential fix or answer to the answer choices and eliminate all that don't match. Most of the choices are legitimate definitions of *liberal*. But you're looking for the correct definition in context. That's exactly why you want to arm yourself with a prediction before you even look at the choices.

E is exactly the opposite of what you're looking for. Eliminate it. (You'll very often see the opposite of what you're looking for in the answer choices.) **A**, **B**, and **C** also do not match the prediction, "broad." **D** works.

Take a moment to double-check your selection. Plug *wide-ranging* back into the sentence as a check:

> *In chapter six, Vitruvius reports that he has had the benefit of a **wide-ranging** Greek education, which he recommends to all aspiring architects.*

Don't forget to do this! It takes a second and can save you a point.

One last note on VICs: When in doubt, eliminate the choice that contains the most common meaning of the word in question. If the most common definition of the word in question were always the correct choice, VICs would not do a very good job of using vocabulary to test your comprehension of the context in which the word appears. The correct choices tend to be less common definitions of the word in question. Therefore, if you're stumped, eliminate the choice that contains the most common meaning—the meaning that would be listed first in the dictionary, so to speak—and go with one of the other choices.

2. Literal Comprehension

The principal function of the fifth paragraph (lines 4–56) is to show

(A) that contemporary architects did not find *On Architecture* helpful to their work
(B) why Vitruvius ended up building so many structures for Augustus
(C) how Vitruvius constructed *On Architecture's* ten chapters with his audience's likely reading habits in mind
(D) that Augustus was as busy as any modern-day executive
(E) how the nature of ancient scrolls discouraged readers

Literal Comprehension questions test whether you understand something specific about the passage—in this case, whether you know what paragraph 5 is doing.

These questions act like mini–research projects. You're told where to go in the passage. The combination of your margin notes, your outline, and a little research will give you the answer.

As with almost all RP questions, knowing the main idea of the passage and taking brief notes will help. Our margin note for paragraph 5 was

O.A. originally scrolls, not book

The scroll-vs.-book point is brought up in support of the author's "mundane" explanation for Vitruvius's treatment of Etruscan temples. (The other point was the résumé-like nature of *On Architecture* as a whole.) Specifically, the physical act of reading scrolls shaped how ancient authors organized their writings. That's our prediction for the answer.

Now let's look at the choices: We don't know that contemporary architects didn't find Vitruvius's book helpful. All the author stated was that architects weren't Vitruvius's primary audience. But, even if the author *had* stated that, it's beside the point: This paragraph is about scrolls, not intended audience. Cut **A**.

B also confuses the passage's main ideas: We don't know whether Vitruvius did end up getting architectural commissions. All we know is that the author maintains that this was what Vitruvius was *trying* to do.

C looks pretty good. Keep it in mind, but take the time to look at *all* the answer choices.

D is a tricky choice because it's a perfectly legitimate inference. But this paragraph is not primarily concerned with Augustus. Rather, it's concerned with Vitruvius.

As for **E**, we don't know that scrolls *discouraged readers*. This is an unwarranted inference playing off the statement that the physical nature of scrolls *encouraged* ancient *authors* to construct their books in a particular fashion.

So **C** is our winner.

3. Attitude

On the whole, the author's attitude toward the traditional scholarly explanation of Vitruvius's description of the Etruscan temple style described in lines 12–34 is one of

(A)   indifference
(B)   respect
(C)   frustration
(D)   interest
(E)   mistrust

Attitude questions focus on the author, particularly the author's attitude or tone toward the subject matter. As you skim and outline an RP, you should always pay attention to the author's tone. In fact, you should underline or circle the words the author uses that indicate his or her tone.

Our sample question asks about the author's tone in a specific place in the passage, so we should answer it first. On test day, you might also see Attitude questions that refer to the author's overarching tone in the entire passage; you should answer Attitude questions about the whole passage last, after you've answered specific questions (like VIC or Literal Comprehension).

Re-reading the referenced lines in the second paragraph shows us that the author felt rather neutral about the explanation. If we read just a smidge beyond the reference lines, to the start of paragraph 3, we see that the author thinks the traditional explanation is pretty good:

Vitruvius's belief that specific natural proportions should be extended to architectural forms does help to explain why he idealized Etruscan temples.

When we tackled the passage, we characterized the author's tone as: *respectfully academic; a discussion*. That characterization holds in this specific instance as well. Once again, the information you gathered by skimming and outlining the passage provides a good prediction to one of the questions with no extra effort required.

Now let's check out the answer choices: In this case, **B** jumps right out. Okay, but let's say you hadn't nailed down the tone as precisely as we did. Let's say all you knew was that the tone was "good" rather than "bad." That's very useful information! You can eliminate any choice that contains a negative word: **A**, **C**, and **E**. Now you have a 50/50 shot at getting a point. Furthermore, you might notice that *interest*, **D**, is not quite specific enough. One could show interest and still take on quite a negative tone. Thus the best choice is **B**.

4. Big Picture/Purpose

The main purpose of the passage is to

(A)   expose Vitruvius's dishonesty
(B)   prove the value of a Greek education
(C)   suggest that Vitruvius considered Etruscan temples to be the most important type of temple
(D)   discuss the differences between ancient scrolls and modern books
(E)   account for the difference between Vitruvius's written description of Etruscan temples and their archaeological remains

We call these "Big Picture/Purpose" questions because they ask you about the passage's major purpose or main idea. These questions vary a little in form, but they're easily identifiable. Phrases like *main idea, primary purpose*, and *main point* identify this question type. Save these general questions for last.

Here's where the Essential Concepts are especially useful. If you read for the author's purpose in the first place, you already have a ready-made potential answer with no extra effort. And if you noted the purpose in your outline, you won't even have to go back to the passage—you can just refer to your notes.

As always, you'll want to generate a potential answer *without* looking at the answer choices. We determined the purpose to be: *To introduce another explanation for why Vitruvius ignored diversity in Etruscan temples.*

Before we settle on an answer choice that resembles our prediction, we want you to notice a couple of things that can help you if you get stuck on test day. First, notice how the first word in each answer choice is a verb:

(A) **expose** Vitruvius's dishonesty
(B) **prove** the value of a Greek education
(C) **suggest** that Vitruvius considered Etruscan temples to be the most important type of temple
(D) **discuss** the differences between ancient scrolls and modern books
(E) **account** for the difference between Vitruvius's written description of Etruscan temples and their archaeological remains

Look for the verb that most closely matches your summary of author's purpose. You can eliminate **A** immediately because it doesn't match the passage's tone. Remember: Answer choices with extreme language tend to be incorrect.

B is a distortion. Because so many distractors boil down to distortions of the text, it's worth teasing out exactly how this nasty little distractor works. Frequently, distractors mix up beliefs that the *author* holds with beliefs held by the people *the author discusses*. In the passage, the author mentions that *Vitruvius* valued a Greek education. The author's opinion is neither stated nor relevant. The reason the author mentions a Greek education is to present the traditional scholarly interpretation of Vitruvius's treatment of Etruscan temples. If you were pressed for time, you might have grabbed for **B** simply because it "looks familiar." That's how RP distractors seduce you, so be warned!

C is another typical distractor. It states the opposite of what the passage states. The author noted that the fact that Vitruvius buried his discussion of Etruscan temples at the end of a book (i.e., scroll) most likely means that Vitruvius *didn't* think it very important. (By the way, whether you agree with that judgment isn't important—what matters is what the author thinks. This is true of all RPs. Not only must you keep the author's beliefs separate from the beliefs of the people he discusses, but you must also keep your *own* opinions out of it as well. You're being tested on how much you can gather from the text, not what you know about the topic.)

As for **D**, it's true that the author discusses the differences between ancient scrolls and modern books. But that's not the *main purpose* of the passage. This distractor tries to pass a supporting notion off as the main purpose of the passage.

E matches the prediction very nicely. That statement encompasses the entire passage. It includes both the discussion of the traditional explanation and the author's own complementary explanation.

But notice one thing choices **B**, **C**, and **D** have in common. Each of them puts forward a subordinate or secondary feature of the passage as the *main* overarching purpose or point. Because you know that this is a Big Picture question, a subordinate feature of the passage can't be right.

5. Inference

The author would most likely agree that the physical form of ancient books

(A)   prevented ancient authors from writing as well as modern authors

(B)   encouraged the writing of encyclopedic overviews

(C)   was responsible for the spread of ancient knowledge

(D)   is a unique source of insight into ancient writing largely ignored by
       traditional scholars

(E)   undermined the ability of ancient authors to gain patrons

Inference questions ask for *implied information*. They want you to take a piece of information given in the passage and use it to figure out something else. Because the answers are not given explicitly within the passage, these questions are often significantly more difficult than specific detail questions. But they're just as common, so you need to get a handle on them. These tend to be general questions in the sense that Inference questions require you to understand the *entire* passage, even if the question refers to a specific part of that passage, as in our example. Save them for last.

An *inference* is best understood as an unobserved fact that one believes must be true given other observed facts. For example:

FACTS	INFERENCE
When I went to sleep last night, there was no snow on the ground.	It snowed while I was asleep.
When I woke up this morning, there was snow on the ground.	

Some inferences are not as logically necessary as the snow example. They are merely statistically possible or logically probable. Take a look at these examples:

Fact: *Most of the school's students had complained that the dress code was too strict.*

Fact: *The new principal changed the dress code to make it less strict.*

Inference: *Student complaints led to the change in the dress code.*

Well, that *might* be the case. The reasoning used to infer that student complaints led to the policy change makes sense. But there are other possible reasons, each of which is based on a hidden assumption:

Hidden Assumption 1: *The school's administration takes student complaints into account.*
Other Potential Reason: *Parents complained on behalf of their children. The school's administration took these complaints more seriously.*

Hidden Assumption 2: *The new principal changed the policy in response to student complaints rather than out of his own preexisting beliefs.*
Other Potential Reason: *The new principal believes that what students wear doesn't have much of an impact on how they learn.*

Hidden Assumption 3: *The new code reflects student concerns.*
Other Potential Reason: *Maybe the dress code is technically less strict but not in the ways that mattered to the students.*

Many questions will ask you to make an inference based on the information given in the passage. You'll need to decide which inferences are valid and which are not. Proper inferences tend to be closer to the snow example than to the dress code example—that is, more logically necessary than statistically probable. Inference questions frequently use verbs such as *suggest*, *infer, imply*, and *indicate*. When asked for an inference, most test takers will pick something that might be possible, and perhaps even suggested, but that doesn't technically qualify as an inference. Always look for the strongest support from the text for any inference you make.

When you're dealing with Inference questions, it's difficult to precisely predict what the answer will be. However, these possibilities are limited by the RP's topic, scope, purpose, and main idea. Here, for example, any inference we make will be limited by the specific function that the scroll-form of ancient books plays in this passage.

To answer this question, step back and remind yourself of what this function was. In our margin notes we wrote, *O.A. originally scrolls, not book.* Now would be a good time to go back to where scrolls are discussed and re-read. We'll reproduce that paragraph here:

> *Moreover, one must also keep in mind that* On Architecture, *like all ancient books, was originally published as a series of scrolls. Each modern "chapter" most likely corresponds to one ancient scroll. This physical form lent even greater significance to the snappy, pertinent introductions and the concise writing that modern readers also demand. The physical act of reading a scroll made the kind of flipping back and forth that modern paginated books allow significantly more inconvenient. Scrolls strongly encouraged ancient authors to front-load the most important ideas they wanted to convey. The ancient author had to earn each "unrolling" by concentrating that much more on the order in which ideas were presented and the economy with which they were expressed—and how much more so when one's intended audience is the emperor of Rome?*

The main point is that scrolls made ancient writers more mindful than modern writers of the organization and presentation of their ideas because reading a scroll was a bit more inconvenient than reading a modern book. So our answer choice should somehow reflect this point.

Let's take a look at the choices: **A** is an unwarranted inference. We simply don't know what the author thought because he gives no hint of a preference between ancient and modern writers.

B is the opposite of what the passage states. Scrolls forced ancient writers to put the most important information at the beginning of their "chapters" and *discouraged* including unnecessary detail.

C is what we refer to as a "left-field" choice. The cause of the spread of ancient knowledge is outside the scope of the passage.

D looks pretty good. The author presents the scroll-nature of ancient books as a novel source of insight into the content and structure of ancient writing, and specifically Vitruvius's *On Architecture*. Although the author accepts the validity of the traditional scholarly interpretation, which is based on Vitruvius's adherence to Greek philosophy, the author's purpose is to present a new and different, but complementary, explanation based on more "mundane" considerations.

E is a typical distortion. Sure, the passage argues that the desire to gain Augustus as a patron drove Vitruvius's writing. But this point is completely separate from the nature of writing for scrolls, as opposed to modern books. Distractors like these merely associate terms and concepts from the passage in order to lure you into making a mistake. **D** is correct.

SPECIAL ADVICE FOR FICTION

Fiction passages will *only* appear as Long RPs. That said, there's no guarantee that you'll see fiction on test day.

If you do see a fiction RP, remember that the only major difference between fiction and nonfiction passages is that fiction passages are not structured as rigidly as nonfiction passages are. When reading a fiction RP, keep the following question in mind: "Who is doing what to whom and how does it make everyone, including the narrator, feel?"

To brush up on your understanding of literary techniques, take a look at our recap of fiction's main elements, any or all of which might show up in the questions that follow the fiction passage:

- **The narrator:** The "voice" that's telling the story.
- **The characters.** Keep in mind who's who, and what their relationships are (mother/daughter, friends, husband/wife, etc.).
- **The plot.** Not much can actually transpire in a passage of roughly 850 words. Events will be apparent. The most you'll be asked to do is read between the lines of what characters say to one another, which is a skill you already use every day. ("Jane said I look good today. Does she really mean this, or was it a sarcastic dig?")
- **The way the author uses language to convey states of mind and events.** Looking for this is like identifying the author's purpose in nonfiction passages.

As you read, circle names of characters, key dialogue, crucial images—anything that keeps you physically and mentally engaged. Aim to get an idea of what happens where in the passage so that when you hit the questions you'll have some idea of where you might need to go in the passage to puzzle out a particular item.

PRACTICE SET

Our practice set contains a Long RP, Short RP, and Paired RP. If you're short on time, skip the Long RP and head straight to the Short and Paired RPs.

Questions 1–6 are based on the following passage.

This passage is from a 2003 novel about a young woman named Angela who at age eight left China with her family to move to San Francisco.

Line
Our parents had known each other in China; we'd even taken the same boat to America. However, within five years of our arrival in San Francisco, Norman and I had become strangers. Relatives already established in the city helped Norman's parents assimilate. Within a year, they had not only learned English,
5   but had also become real estate moguls. I learned all this from the Chinese American gossip machine that constantly tabulated every family's level of success. The machine judged my family lacking. My parents ran a grocery store and, unlike Norman's family, gravitated to the immigrant subculture. They never learned English, but they respected that I tamed that beast of a language. I was
10   my parents' communication link with the "outside world."

My parents denied themselves in order to ensure that I could attend Baywood, a top private high school. That was where Norman and I crossed paths again. However much my relative mastery of English had elevated my status at home, at Baywood I remained a shy and brainy outsider. Norman was very popular: he
15   played football and was elected class president. He and gorgeous Judy Kim were named King and Queen of the Winter Ball; their portrait adorned every available bulletin board. I scoffed at the celebrity silently. Back then, I did everything silently. Compared to Norman, who had already achieved the American teenage ideal, I was anonymous. From the sidelines I observed his triumphs with barely
20   acknowledged envy. In May of our freshman year, Norman approached me after our chemistry class.

"Hey, Angela," he said as my heart leapt into my throat. "I missed class a couple of days ago. Can I copy your notes?" "Sure," I said. I was horrified to find myself blushing. We soon became study buddies. It was all business—no small
25   talk beyond the necessary niceties. But the hours we piled up studying together generated an unspoken mutual respect and an unacknowledged intimacy. Judy noticed this and took an increasing dislike to me. This relationship continued throughout high school.

One day in eleventh grade, without looking up from the math problem he was
30   working on, Norman asked: "What schools are you applying to?"

It was the first time he had shown any real personal interest in me. "Berkeley, if I'm lucky," I said.

"You could probably get in anywhere."

"What do you mean?"

He looked up from his math problem and met my gaze.

"Berkeley is just across the bay. Don't you want to experience something new for once? I'm applying to schools back East," he said. "You should, too."

Not for the first time, an exciting vision of ivy-covered walls and perhaps even a new identity swept over me and was almost immediately subsumed by a wave of guilt.

"But what about my parents?"

"But what about *you*?"

Norman had broken a taboo. I launched into a self-righteous refutation of the possibility he had dared to voice. I told him that even though I wasn't popular and my family wasn't as successful as his, I at least hadn't forgotten that it was my parents who had brought me here and who had struggled so much for me. How could I make them unhappy?

Norman had expected this outburst. He smiled. "We're not so different, you know. We started out in the same boat. Now we're in the same boat again." He laughed. "We've always been in the same boat. Our parents might be kind of different, but they want us to succeed and be happy."

"You're so American," I said in a tone hovering between approval and reproach. "You're not even worried about leaving your parents to go to school back East."

"That's not what being American means," he insisted.

"Well, what does it mean, then?" I demanded. Surely, I, and not this superficial football player who needed my academic help, knew what it meant to be American. That very day I had received an A on my American History term paper.

"It means, Angela," he said gently, "that our parents brought us here so we could have the freedom to figure out for ourselves what to do with our lives."

He smiled at my speechlessness and then returned to his math problem.

Without looking up from his notebook, he said, "If I can decide to go to school back East, so can you."

1. What is the purpose of the information in the first sentence?

(A) To show Angela and Norman's similar histories so as to emphasize their current differences

(B) To emphasize that both Angela and Norman have come a long way since their childhoods in China

(C) To let the reader know that Angela came from a poor family that could not afford to fly to America

(D) To make the reader think that Norman and Angela will inevitably become friends

(E) To let the reader see how highly Angela values her family's history

2. The word "tabulated" in line 6 emphasizes that

(A) the other Chinese immigrants were very aware of who was succeeding in a material way and who was not

(B) Angela's neighbors calculated the exact amount of money her family was earning

(C) Norman's family checked the prices of everything they owned

(D) Angela lived in a poor section of San Francisco

(E) Angela was determined to earn more money than Norman

3. The use of italics in line 49 serves to emphasize

(A) Norman's unrealistic desire to go to school outside of California

(B) Norman's idealistic goals as contrasted with Angela's lack of ambition

(C) Norman's concern that Angela has not thought about her own educational desires

(D) the small chance that Angela will accomplish her dreams

(E) the degree to which Angela has undermined her potential

4. In line 52, Angela uses the word "American" to differentiate between

(A) concern for the future and fear of failure

(B) personal ambition and responsibility to one's parents

(C) imagination and conservatism

(D) duty to family and duty to friends

(E) love for adventure and love for travel

5. Throughout the passage, the main focus is on

(A) the awkwardness Angela feels knowing that Norman already has a girlfriend
(B) Angela's ambition to do well in school and get into a good college
(C) the challenges Angela faces living in America while feeling like an outsider
(D) Angela's excitement over getting an A on her history term paper
(E) how personal ambition is the key to getting ahead in America

6. From details in the passage, it is clear that

(A) Angela went ahead with her plan to attend Berkeley
(B) Angela grew to be more outspoken
(C) Norman went on to play football in college
(D) Angela decided to go to college back East
(E) Angela majored in math at college

Questions 7–9 are based on the following passage.

Line   One of the features that distinguish traditional Pueblo pottery from other types
of clay art is the absence of machinery from all parts of the creative process.
The clay is gathered, processed, and finally shaped by hand. Instead of using a
potter's wheel to create vases and other round objects, the Pueblo pottery artist
5   rolls clay into long pieces and then painstakingly coils them into layers of circles.
Paints are produced from plants and minerals found near the Pueblo village and
applied with a handmade brush fashioned from a yucca cactus.

    This adherence to tradition is one of the things that makes Pueblo pottery so
attractive to the art collector. Since the Pueblo potter shuns techniques of mass
10   production, the collector can be sure that every piece of Pueblo clay art is uniquely
shaped. This quality also makes examples of Pueblo pottery excellent gifts.

7. According to information provided in the passage, what change to the Pueblo
pottery production process would do most to make examples of Pueblo pottery
LESS attractive as gifts?

(A) Substitution of synthetic paints for the natural pigments currently used
(B) Changes to the way the clay is gathered and processed
(C) Changes to the type of clay used
(D) The replacement of traditional Pueblo decoration with more modern designs
(E) The introduction of molds to guarantee uniform size and shape

8. The function of the first paragraph is to

(A) establish a thesis that will be refuted in the second paragraph
(B) establish a thesis that will be supported in the second paragraph
(C) provide information that will be used to explain a phenomenon discussed in the second paragraph
(D) present two differing opinions about Pueblo pottery
(E) explain why it is important for people interested in collecting art to learn about Pueblo pottery

9. According to information provided in the passage, what change would do MOST to threaten future production of traditional Pueblo pottery?

(A) The replacement of the traditional process with standardized technology
(B) The increase in popularity of Pueblo pottery
(C) A loss in interest in Pueblo pottery on the part of art collectors
(D) A reduction in the number of Pueblo pottery pieces given as gifts each year
(E) The introduction of new styles of pottery similar to Pueblo pottery

Questions 10–20 are based on the following passages.

On January 14, 2004, President George W. Bush announced a reorganization of NASA resources to make a manned mission to Mars the agency's primary goal. This announcement reignited a long-smoldering debate on manned space travel. These passages, adapted from recently published articles, discuss the advisability of further American investment in manned space travel.

Passage 1

Line
The popularity of manned space flight stems from a peculiar mixture of American ideals buried deep in the national consciousness. Can-do optimism and engineering know-how combine with a New Frontier to provide something quasi-religious: the chance to be born again by ascending to the heavens.

5   Unprecedented material benefits—the storied "spin-offs" that we're always promised—will doubtlessly emanate from this noble effort that will unify our fractious country. Marshalling America's techno-scientific expertise for a Pilgrimage into space will allow us to re-enact our national origins and renew our appointed role: to create a shining City on a Hill in a New World that

10   presents the last best hope of mankind. Thus, manned space flight reconciles seemingly contradictory aspects of the national identity: nostalgic and forward-looking, religious and scientific, spiritual and material.

Only through the sobering examination of the costs and benefits of 15 manned space flights can the effect of so seductively romantic a brew be shaken off.

15   Should we spend hundreds of billions of dollars on, say, a mission to Mars when

we face crushing problems such as poverty, terrorism, and global warming?
The likely benefits of manned space flight had better be staggering in the face of
the opportunity costs* of not directly investing in problems such as these.

20   Thus, I would like to discuss a non-romantic argument often put forth in favor
of manned space flight. Enthusiasts claim that space-based scientific research
is both invaluable and impossible to replicate on Earth. There is little proof for
this claim. For example, *Mir*, the now-defunct space station, yielded no scientific
break-throughs commensurate with its cost. In one experiment, scientists
concluded that plants did not grow well in space. Clearly, this bit of information

25   would be invaluable only to astronauts. Furthermore, a reexamination of
this experiment found that plant growth had been stunted for quite mundane
and well-understood reasons. Ethylene, a gas long known to be released by
plants, had accumulated in the enclosure and inhibited growth. So much
for invaluable groundbreaking advances. As for important research that can't

30   be accomplished on Earth, it is often argued that the only way to study the
long-term effects of zero-gravity on the human body is in space. This argument
carries weight only for those already committed to manned space flight. But as
an independent argument for manned space flight, this argument is circular: We
must have manned space flight to understand the long-term effects of zero-

35   gravity in order to have more manned space flight.

A sober cost/benefit analysis shows that robotic space exploration trumps
manned space flight. Robots have proven to be remarkably effective at exploring
our solar system. Their scientific impact is ubiquitously acknowledged. In terms
of financial and human cost, robot expeditions are far cheaper to mount.

40   The circularity of even seemingly non-romantic arguments for manned space
flight belies the fundamental romanticism of its supporters. Doubtlessly unaware
of the ingredients in the seductive brew noted above, enthusiasts support manned
space flight because they think it would be really fun and exciting. Being an
American, I can understand this. I, too, yearn for adventures on alien shores. But

45   even though it would be really fun and exciting to deplete all my savings on a
year-long adventure on merely Mediterranean shores, as an adult I know that
I have more pressing, if less enticing, claims on my resources. Those who argue
for manned space flight do so out of romantic, escapist, and childlike notions that
they should outgrow.

Passage 2

50   The orbiting astronaut looks down on his home and grasps both its fragility
and the pettiness of our mundane conflicts. How trite! How dare we spend vast

---

*An "opportunity cost" is a comparison between the likely return on one investment
and the likely return on another.

sums on manned space flight when six billion of us live in the midst of conflicts
and problems, which, perhaps "petty" from a God's-eye view, threaten the future
of our civilization and species? Furthermore, the oft-made assertion that manned
55 space experiments have yielded critical advances either directly or indirectly is
arguable at best.

So goes the fashionable critique of manned space travel. However, rather than
cynically dismiss the astronaut's now-proverbial reaction to seeing the Earth
from on high, I propose that we consider the potential benefits that this change
60 in perspective would have on real-world problems were it only spread more
widely. Moreover, equally intangible "romantic" impulses to explore should
not be thrown aside so lightly. Motivation matters. Where would we be today if
Christopher Columbus had not embarked on his "folly" to open a western
passage to the East? Beneficial unintended consequences—or, "spin-offs"—are
65 real and predate the moon shot. Columbus, in fact, failed to open a new
trade route to the East, but he did find two continents previously unknown
to his contemporaries in Europe, Asia, and Africa. Although clearly not entirely
beneficial—especially for the millions of Native Americans felled by Old-World
diseases or conquistadors' muskets—Columbus' discovery nevertheless made
70 great things possible, such as the United States.

Rather than retreat in embarrassment from the charge of "romanticism,"
we should embrace it. The case for manned space flight should rest explicitly
upon the rejuvenating and unifying potential the effort provides our troubled
world. In particular, we should cease insisting that immensely important
75 scientific discoveries are imminent and inevitable. Although this almost certainly
is the case, we really don't need manned space flight to yield scientific
discoveries; robots do very well for that purpose. Moreover, the real-world
benefits of intangible inspiration are not limited to a welcome and fruitful change
in perspective. How many young people would rush into the sciences if a
80 full-scale global effort in manned space flight—a mission to Mars is the obvious
choice—were launched? How beneficial would the consequences of the requisite
and unprecedented international cooperation be for the grave issues that face our
species here on Earth?

Rather than promise dubious economic boons when we're labeled "escapist,"
85 we should explicitly state the possibility that we have already failed on this
planet and that space is our only long-term option. Most scientists agree that we
are already dangerously close to Earth's carrying capacity. Surely, within the
half-century or so it would take to truly conquer manned space flight, we will
be that much closer to a nightmare of ecological or societal collapse. Doesn't the
90 likely prospect of global collapse in itself represent the most massive opportunity
cost possible for not investing heavily in manned space flight? It's at the very
least arguable that the new frontier of the Americas gave rise to a kind of society

whose ideals truly are the last best hope of mankind. Wouldn't the new frontier
of space bestow another opportunity for fruitful experiments in enlightened
95   government? I maintain that we cannot afford to throw aside the undeniable
romantic appeal that a global effort to put man in space would engender. Our
civilization will need all the help it can get to survive this century. I can think
of no argument for manned space flight more unromantic than that.

10. Which of the following, if true, would most clearly STRENGTHEN the assertion
in Passage 1 about science experiments conducted in space (lines 21–27)?

(A) Many of the recent developments in gene therapy are directly attributed to
experiments conducted on *Mir*.

(B) Recent reports have questioned the objectivity of the critics of the *Mir*
program.

(C) A full report on all experiments conducted in space has yet to be evaluated.

(D) A list of the 100 most important scientific discoveries since the beginning
of manned space travel yielded none based on experiments conducted in
space.

(E) Many of the experiments conducted in space are highly technical, and not
easily accessible to the layman.

11. With which of the following statements would the author of Passage 1 be LEAST
likely to agree?

(A) When considering whether an investment is worthwhile, the likely benefits
of that investment should be weighed against the likely benefits of a
similar investment in another venture.

(B) The benefits of manned space missions do not outweigh the benefits of
robotic space missions to a degree significant enough to justify the higher
cost of the former.

(C) The strong support for manned space missions among Americans is
surprising given the spirituality of the American people.

(D) It is part of the American character to be attracted by the idea of
experiencing exciting adventures in new territories.

(E) Part of becoming an adult is coming to recognize that the potential benefits
of any venture must be weighed against the costs.

12. In line 36, "trumps" most nearly means

    (A) devises
    (B) suits
    (C) duplicates
    (D) outperforms
    (E) defrauds

13. According to Passage 2, the argument that people should not go into space is

    (A) harmlessly entertaining
    (B) unjustly scornful
    (C) logically flawed
    (D) astutely argued
    (E) unnecessarily complicated

14. The author of Passage 2 begins by describing an astronaut's view from space in order to

    (A) emphasize that the astronaut is a kind of national hero
    (B) show how overly simplistic things look in space
    (C) prepare the reader for the idea that new perspectives can be important
    (D) warn the reader against adopting an overly romantic notion of space travel
    (E) prove that environmental problems are so severe that their effects can be seen from space

15. The word "fashionable" in line 57 most nearly means

    (A) flattering
    (B) apparent
    (C) wholesome
    (D) trendy
    (E) conspicuous

16. Which of the following strategies for arguing in favor of manned space missions would the author of Passage 2 be MOST likely to favor?

(A) emphasizing the importance of scientific experiments conducted in space
(B) showing the benefits of traveling to Mars
(C) emphasizing the way it will nurture and inspire positive sentiments in the people back on Earth
(D) proving precisely what discoveries lie in wait for us in space
(E) eliminating the danger of manned space travel

17. Which of the following most accurately describes the last paragraph of Passage 2 in relation to arguments in Passage 1?

(A) The author of Passage 2 proposes a new argument and revives an argument dismissed in Passage 1.
(B) The author of Passage 2 predicts a future series of events also considered in Passage 1.
(C) The author of Passage 2 examines an idea from Passage 1 and disputes the figures offered in support.
(D) The author of Passage 2 asserts a viewpoint shared by the author of Passage 1 by offering up historical evidence.
(E) The author of Passage 2 reconciles his point of view with the author of Passage 1.

18. In each passage, the author assumes that the efficacy of scientific experiments conducted in space is

(A) useful only if carefully monitored by a mirror crew on the ground
(B) called into question only by the most cynical of observers
(C) tragically underutilized by the most talented scientists
(D) only justifiable under certain circumstances
(E) not enough to justify manned space flight

19. The passages differ in their evaluation of manned space flight in that Passage 1 claims that

    (A)   space enthusiasts ultimately want to go to the moon for romantic notions

    (B)   propagandists have falsified the data of scientific experiments to justify their continued use

    (C)   the only real benefits of manned space travel could be achieved less expensively with robotic space exploration

    (D)   Christopher Columbus had a specific goal in mind when he set off on his journey

    (E)   the only way to understand the long-term impact of space travel on the body is to engage in manned space flights

20. Both passages are primarily concerned with

    (A)   the poor planning of current space missions

    (B)   the future of manned space flight

    (C)   the eventuality of going to Mars

    (D)   the best way to improve the space program

    (E)   the introduction of more math and science into the school curriculum

Guided Explanations

1. A

This is a fiction Long RP. We're going to assume that you forced yourself to focus, skimmed, and took notes in the margins as a way of outlining the passage. We're also going to assume that you identified the main characters, circled key dialogue, and jotted down a few notes about the plot. (If you didn't, go back and review our fiction section on page 164.

This specific Literal Comprehension question asks you to identify the purpose of the first sentence. It's a little bit tricky because the question requires you to think about a particular sentence in relation to the passage as a whole. Begin by taking a look at the specific lines: The first sentence informs the reader that Angela's parents and Norman's parents knew one another in China and that the two young people came across on the same boat. This common history contrasts with and thereby draws attention to their differences. These differences provide the passage with its tension and interest. The other answers all offer details that may be true to a certain extent, but none is as important to the entire passage.

2. A

Another specific question—this time, a VIC question. The word *tabulated* appears in the passage to express what *the Chinese American gossip machine* does with regard to *every family's success*. This involves keeping a record of that success and comparing it to the success of other Chinese American families. Remember to predict an answer and avoid choices that present straight dictionary definitions (VICs test just that: vocabulary *in context*). **B** is tempting because the word *tabulated* sounds like and is occasionally used to mean "calculated," but in this context comparisons of status are more germane than exact calculations of salaries.

3.   C

This specific Literal Comprehension question points you to a particular place in the passage. As always, you should review a few lines above and a few lines below the particular line given in the question. Angela responds to Norman's suggestion that she think about applying to East Coast colleges with the question *What about my parents?* because she thinks it would be wrong to move far away from her mother and father. Norman, however, thinks it would be worse for Angela to put concern for her parents ahead of her own educational ambitions, and the word *you* is italicized to express his desire that Angela should consider her own interests first.

4.   B

Another specific VIC question. Taking a look at the referenced lines tells us that Angela clarifies her remark that Norman is so *American* by telling him, *You're not even worried about leaving your parents to go to school back East*. Angela is shocked that Norman would put his personal ambition (to attend an Eastern college) before his responsibilities to his parents (which would entail going to school close to their home on the West Coast).

5.   C

At long last, a general Big Picture/Purpose question question asking about the passage's topic and scope ("main focus"), which hopefully you saved for last. The main idea of the first paragraph is that Angela's family never assimilated into American culture the way Norman's did and was even judged as insufficient by the *Chinese American gossip machine*. In the second paragraph, the reader learns that Angela felt like an outsider at high school, despite her success in learning English. Finally, in the conversation with Norman, Angela realizes that her study partner may know more about what it means to be American, regardless of the A she got on her American History paper, and she begins to understand that she has never considered taking advantage of the freedom to choose that her parents provided her by bringing her to America. Throughout the passage, Angela feels that she is alienated from her surroundings in one way or another. The other choices are details of the passage, or distortions of those details.

6. B

Another general question, which asks you to *infer* something about the passage. It's tricky because the question asks you something about the future. Remember, *Angela*—an older, wiser Angela—is the narrator. In lines 17–18, Angela remarks that *back then, I did everything silently*. The phrase *back then* indicates that doing everything silently is something Angela overcame later in life and that she became more outspoken. Although Norman's suggestion that she could attend an Eastern college clearly made an impact on Angela, it is not clear from the passage whether she decided to follow up on this idea or stick with her plan to attend Berkeley, so answers **A** and **D** are incorrect. There is no indication that Angela went on to major in math or that Norman continued to play football, so **C** and **E** are incorrect. That leaves **B**, the correct answer.

7. E

We're going to assume that you quickly checked out the questions before reading this Short RP on pottery. Reviewing the questions before reading the short passage lets you focus your attention and make a prediction about the correct answer. The last sentence of the passage asserts that it is the uniqueness of Pueblo pottery pieces that makes them attractive as gifts. If molds were introduced to the production process to guarantee uniform size and shape, this uniqueness would be lost, and pieces of Pueblo pottery would be less attractive as gifts. So we need an answer that deals with the "loss of uniqueness." **A** and **D** are tempting because they propose changes that would seem likely to make Pueblo pottery more *modern* and thus possibly less attractive for gift giving, but the passage connects the artwork's popularity among gift givers to the unique shape of each piece.

8. C

This is a Literal Comprehension question: The correct answer will explain the function of the first paragraph. We might make a prediction along the lines of "it explains how each piece of Pueblo pottery is shaped and painted by hand." This, in turn, explains the uniqueness of Pueblo pottery, which is the focus of the second paragraph. So we need an answer that demonstrates this relationship. **E** doesn't link the first and second paragraphs, so cut that choice. The first paragraph doesn't present a thesis, so **A** and **B** are out. That leaves **C** and **D**: **C** correctly explains the relationship.

9. A

This Inference question asks us to make a prediction based on the information provided in the passage. Remember to always answer this type of question after you've tackled the specific questions. Pueblo pottery is defined by its hand-wrought nature. The introduction of standardized technology would threaten the production of *traditional* Pueblo pottery. **A** matches our prediction, so that's the answer. The changes proposed in **B**, **C**, **D**, and **E** might all reduce *demand* for Pueblo pottery, but this would not necessarily threaten production (there is no suggestion that the primary motivation for the production of Pueblo pottery is commercial).

10. D

According to the Paired RP Step Method, each passage needs to be considered separately, as if it were a long, Long RP. This means that each passage needs to be skimmed and outlined. We also need to answer the questions dealing with Passage 1 first (10–12), then answer the questions dealing with

Passage 2 (13–16), and finally answer the questions dealing with both passages (17–20). Last but not least, within each group of questions, specific questions should be tackled first, followed by general questions.

This question requires you to *infer* something about a particular part of the passage. Passage 1 asserts that scientific experiments conducted in space do not yield results important enough to offset their costs, so the correct answer will offer an argument supporting this idea. If it were true that none of the 100 most important scientific discoveries since the beginning of manned space travel was conducted in space, this fact would certainly strengthen the position presented in the first passage. That's **D**. The other answers are weakeners.

11. C

This Inference question requires some re-reading. In lines 2–4, the author asserts that the idea of sending people into space to explore new frontiers is "quasi-religious" and appeals to the desire to be born again in the heavens; the author seems convinced that the spirituality of Americans is a driving force behind support for the space program. Our answer needs to contradict these assertions. **C** is the correct answer because the author wouldn't be surprised by such an idea. The other answers all offer statements with which the author would certainly agree, given details and arguments in the passage.

12. D

A straight-up VIC question. In the context of the passage, the word *trumps* is being used to describe the way robotic space exploration is more effective than or *outperforms* manned space flight. None of the words offered in the other answer choices makes sense in the context of the passage. When you're given specific line numbers, always read a few lines before and a few lines after.

13.   B

It's time to focus on Passage 2. This is a tone question. The abrasive language the author uses to articulate the argument against manned space travel (*How trite! How dare we . . . ?*), and the fact that the reader is cautioned against *cynically* dismissing the astronaut's perspective indicate that this argument is regarded as being *unjustly scornful*. **C**, *logically flawed*, is tempting, but the passage disputes the logic against manned space travel showing that supposedly *romantic* arguments in favor of it are actually morbidly hard-headed: *Our civilization will need all the help it can get to survive this century. I can think of no argument for manned space flight more unromantic than that.* There is no evidence to suggest that any of the assessments offered by the other answer choices is accurate.

14.   C

This Literal Comprehension question asks about the purpose of a particular feature in the passage. Note: The purpose of a particular feature won't contradict the overall purpose of the passage. In the second paragraph, the author expresses the idea that the astronaut's experience of seeing the Earth from space grants a new perspective on earthly affairs that might be beneficial if it were spread more widely across the population. **B** and **D** are both tempting because within the first paragraph it appears that the author is criticizing the importance people attach to the astronaut's unique view of the world. Reading the paragraph in the context of the entire passage reveals that the author is writing ironically, however, and is actually objecting to the way people tend to scoff at this enlightening experience.

15.   D

Another specific VIC question. The word *fashionable* is applied to the prevailing view of manned space travel against which the author of Passage 2 is arguing. This view is obviously popular at the time of writing (otherwise the author would not need to address it), so *trendy* is the best meaning. *Flattering* is incorrect because the prevailing view is clearly negative, and *apparent, wholesome,* or *conspicuous* do not make sense in context.

16. C

This question asks us to *infer* something about the author of Passage 2, specifically whether he or she would find certain strategies appealing. At the end of the first paragraph, the author acknowledges that the scientific benefits of manned space missions are debatable. The next paragraph counters this point by arguing that manned space flights are the product of an impulse to explore, which should be nurtured, given that it led to the discovery of the Americas. And the third paragraph asserts that such missions would foster beneficial sentiments of curiosity and cooperativeness. The author clearly sees nurturing and inspiring positive sentiments as among the greatest benefits of manned space flight. The other answers are incorrect because they either contradict the argument of the passage (in the case of **A**) or deal with details not considered in the passage (as in the case of **B**, **D**, and **E**).

17. A

The final few questions following a Paired RP will always deal with the relationship between both passages. Save these questions for last, after you've already answered questions on the individual passages.

This question asks us to compare and contrast by considering a paragraph of Passage 2 in light of the argument put forth in Passage 1. Let your notes guide you here. In the final paragraph, the author of Passage 2 introduces the new argument that manned space travel may become essential as life on Earth becomes unbearable, then makes a case for the idea (dismissed in Passage 1 when the author describes how to *shake off* the effects of the *romantic brew*) that the creation of a New Frontier will provide opportunities for social experimentation and hope for enlightened government. **B** is tempting because the author does predict societal and environmental collapse, but this situation is not considered in Passage 1. **D** is also attractive because the author refers to early American history, but the relevant idea about the New Frontier is clearly not shared by the author of the first passage. The author of Passage 2 neither disputes figures offered in Passage 1 (there are none to dispute) nor reconciles his viewpoint with that of its author, so **C** and **E** are incorrect.

18. E

This question asks us to compare *the efficacy of scientific experiments* described in the two passages. The author of Passage 1 argues extensively for the idea that the scientific discoveries of manned space missions are only useful for future manned space missions, and the author of Passage 2, who proposes other benefits, nevertheless does nothing to refute the idea that the scientific advances yielded by manned space experiments are *arguable at best*. None of the other answers offers an opinion expressed by either author.

19. C

The question asks for a way in which the passages differ in their evaluation of manned space flight, so the right answer must offer a distinction between the two passages that has a bearing on their differing stances regarding sending people into space. **C** is the only answer that meets this requirement— the author of Passage 1 dismisses the romantic benefits of manned space travel and notes that the scientific benefits can be realized by robotic missions at a lower cost. **A** looks attractive at first because criticism of the romantic nature of support for manned space flight is a major element in the first passage's argument; however, both passages acknowledge that there are romantic motivations behind manned space travel, and the second passage merely differs by understanding this as a good thing rather than a problem.

B is incorrect because the author of Passage 1 never claims that the scientific findings were falsified, merely that they are relevant only to further manned missions. **D** is incorrect because Columbus is only mentioned in the second passage. **E** is incorrect because only the first passage mentions the impact of space travel on humans, and actually dismisses it as being of use only to future manned space missions.

20. B

To answer this Big Picture question, we need to compare the central thrust of each passage: Both passages focus on arguments concerning the future of manned space flight. Note that both passages draw a distinction between manned and unmanned missions to space. **A** is incorrect because neither passage criticizes the planning of current space missions, though the first passage questions the need for those missions that carry humans into space. **C** and **E** are incorrect because they offer details from the passages, not their shared focus. **D** is incorrect because both passages focus on one specific aspect of the space program—manned missions, and not the space program in general. This answer is too broad.

INTENSIVE 5

Math Section:
Multiple–Choice &
Grid-In Questions

Math X-ray

Essential Concepts

Essential Strategies

Special Advice for Grid-Ins

Practice Set

THE GOOD NEWS ABOUT SAT MATH IS THAT THE MATH tested on the SAT isn't any harder than what you've already seen in your high school math classes. Here are the major math topics you'll see:

- Arithmetic
- Algebra
- Geometry
- Data Analysis, Statistics, and Probability

Rather than bog you down with every possible equation, formula, or math concept on the SAT, this Intensive gives you the strategies you'll use to solve SAT Math problems. Every practice problem points out the math concepts in play and puts them in **bold**. However, if you do come across a concept you don't know, or you need a refresher, look it up at **www.sparknotes.com/math/primer**. Our online math primer is a resource to help you study any and all topics you may need to review.

Now let's turn our attention to the X-ray, where we'll take a look at sample questions and directions.

MATH X-RAY

On test day, you'll see 44 multiple-choice questions and 10 grid-ins. This section will show you examples of both.

Multiple Choice

<u>Directions for Multiple Choice</u>: Answer each question, using any available space for notes or figuring.

<u>Notes</u>:

1.The use of a calculator is permitted. All numbers used are real numbers.

2. Figures that accompany problems in this test are intended to provide information useful in solving the problems. They are drawn as accurately as possible EXCEPT when it is stated in a specific problem that the figure is not drawn to scale. All figures lie in a plane unless otherwise indicated.

3. Unless otherwise specified, the domain of any function f is assumed to be the set of all real numbers x for which $f(x)$ is a real number.

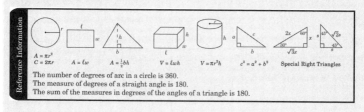

The number of degrees of arc in a circle is 360.
The measure of degrees of a straight angle is 180.
The sum of the measures in degrees of the angles of a triangle is 180.

You might think the SAT gives you a reference area because it asks lots of questions on these topics. Well, you're right. But to avoid getting bogged down on test day, flipping back and forth between questions and the reference area, you should memorize the formulas now. The mathematical facts and rules in the reference area are the foundation for almost every geometry question on the test.

The rest of the directions are straightforward: Read the question, do the math, pick the right answer. In the Essential Strategies section, we'll talk more about when to use your calculator and, most important, how to solve the problems.

Here's a sample multiple-choice question:

A classroom contains 31 chairs, some of which have arms and some of which do not. If the room contains 5 more armchairs than chairs without arms, how many armchairs does it contain?

(A)   10
(B)   13
(C)   16
(D)   18
(E)   21

There are no surprises here in terms of format. You get a question followed by five answer choices. One choice is correct; the other four are distractors. Math distractors tend either to repeat numbers from the problem or give a number you derive along the way to the right answer choice. The correct answer here, by the way, is **D**.

You should be aware that when the answer choices contain numbers (as in this example), as opposed to variables such as $x, y, n,$ or m, the answer choices always appear in either ascending or descending order. This knowledge will come in handy later in this Intensive, when we discuss the Working Backward approach to solving SAT Math questions.

Grid-Ins

The second type of SAT Math question is what we call "grid-ins" because you have to *grid-in* the answer yourself. There are no answer choices from which to choose. A typical grid-in Math question, complete with directions, looks like this:

Directions:

The following questions require you to solve the problem and enter your answer by marking the ovals in the special grid as shown in the examples below.

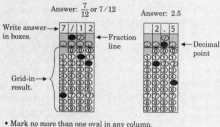

- Mark no more than one oval in any column.

- Because the answer sheet will be machine-scored, **you will receive credit only if the ovals are filled in completely.**

- Although not required, it is suggested that you write your answer in the boxes at the top of the columns to help you fill in the ovals accurately.

- Some problems may have more than one correct answer. In such cases, grid only one answer.

- No question has a negative answer.

- **Mixed numbers** such as $2\frac{1}{2}$ must be gridded as 2.5 or 5/2. If $2\,1\,/\,2$ is gridded, it will be interpreted as $\frac{21}{2}$, not $2\frac{1}{2}$.)

- **Decimal Accuracy:** If you obtain a decimal answer, **enter the most accurate value the grid will accommodate.** For example, if you obtain an answer such as 0.6666 . . . , you should record the result as .666 or .667. **Less accurate values such as .66 or .67 are not acceptable.** Acceptable ways to grid $\frac{2}{3}$ = .666 . . .

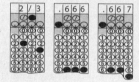

Note: You may start your answers in any column, space permitting. Columns not needed should be left blank.

The original price of a banana in a store is $2. During a sale, the store reduces the price by 25%, and Joe buys the banana. Joe then raises the price of the banana 10% from the price at which he bought it and sells it to Sam. How much does Sam pay for the banana?

Unlike every other question type on the SAT, grid-in questions require you to come up with your own answer. You'll enter your answer by filling in the grid like the one shown above. Notice that ovals representing decimal points and fraction bars are provided in case your answer is not a whole number.

The answer to our sample grid-in is **$1.70** (note that you would only grid-in the *numbers* on test day, not the *dollar sign*). We'll show you how we got it later in this chapter. Now, let's move on to the Essential Concepts.

Math questions appear in order of difficulty. Remember to tackle the easy questions before moving on to the harder ones.

ESSENTIAL CONCEPTS

Later in this Intensive we'll present a step method that you should employ on every Math question you face. However, because different problems call for different approaches, one of the steps, "Plan the Attack," is open-ended and calls for you to choose the most effective approach to the problem at hand. So before we get to the step method itself, we'll first demonstrate a standard approach to SAT Math, as well as a few alternative approaches that may come in handy in particular situations. Therefore, we'll cover the following here:

1. Standard Applications of Math Concepts
2. Alternative Approaches for Special Cases

Essential Concept #1: Standard Applications of Math Concepts

Some questions require nothing more than straightforward applications of the math concepts you learned in junior high or high school. This doesn't necessarily mean that such questions will be easy. Some of the concepts themselves can be complex, and the test makers occasionally complicate matters by sprinkling traps among the choices.

Easier questions often require the application of a single concept, whereas harder questions may involve multiple concepts. Some may even require you to draw your own diagram when none is given. Regardless of the difficulty level, the standard application approach is the same: Scope out the situation, decide on what concept or concepts are being tested, and then use what you know about those concepts to answer the question before looking at the choices. If you've done your work well, the answer you get will be among the choices in the booklet, and you'll bubble it in and move on.

Let's look at a few examples spanning various difficulty levels. We'll work through single-concept questions based on one particular math concept and multiple-concept questions that require you to make use of many bits of math knowledge to arrive at the answer.

SINGLE-CONCEPT QUESTIONS

Here's an example of the simplest kind of math question you'll see:

What is the value of x if $3x - 27 = 33$?

(A) 2
(B) 11
(C) 20
(D) 27
(E) 35

The math concept in play here is **equations with one variable***, which is something you likely remember from algebra class. There's nothing to do here but apply the concept: First isolate the variable by adding 27 to both sides to get $3x = 60$, and then divide both sides by 3 to get $x = 20$, **C**. No doubt the test makers include 2 among the answer choices to trap people who accidentally *subtracted* 27 from both sides, yielding $3x = 6$ and $x = 2$. **B**, 11, is what you get if you divide one number in the problem (33) by another (3), and 27, **D**, appears in the problem itself. Assuming you didn't fall for any of these traps, there's not much to it: Just apply a single, fairly basic concept directly to the problem to pick up the point.

Not all single-concept questions are necessarily so straightforward, however, especially as you get on in the section. Try this one on for size:

At a local golf club, 75 members attend weekday lessons, 12 members attend weekend lessons, and 4 members attend both weekday and weekend lessons. If 10 members of the organization do not attend any lessons, how many members are in the club?

(A) 65
(B) 75
(C) 82
(D) 93
(E) 101

There's only one concept in play here, but if you don't know it, you're in for a very tough time of it. You need the formula for **group problems with two groups: group 1 + group 2 – both + neither = total**. If we let *group 1* be the 75 members who attend weekday lessons and let *group 2* be the 12 members

---

*Again, if this or any other math concept trips you up, go online to **www.sparknotes. com/math/primer** and look it up on our math primer. Every math concept you need to know is covered.

who attend weekend lessons, we get: 75 + 12 – 4 + 10 = *total*. Solving for *total* gives 93, **D**. Notice how **B**, 75, is a number contained in the problem, and **E**, 101, is what you get if you mistakenly *add* 4 instead of *subtract* it.

MULTIPLE-CONCEPT QUESTIONS

Some questions require you to pull together two or more choice tidbits from your math arsenal. One of the most common examples of a multiple-concept question involves geometric formulas that generate equations that need to be solved arithmetically and/or algebraically. Here's an example:

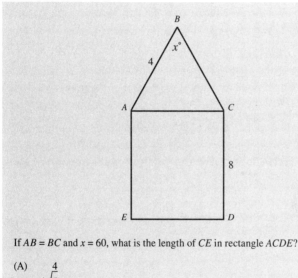

If $AB = BC$ and $x = 60$, what is the length of CE in rectangle $ACDE$?

(A) $\dfrac{4}{}$

(B) $4\sqrt{5}$

(C) $5\sqrt{2}$

(D)   8

(E)   12

This question is a bit more involved than a typical single-concept question because there are a number of geometry concepts you need to know and some genuine opportunities to slip up on the arithmetic end too. It's also what we call a "mish-mash problem" because it involves several shapes: three triangles and a rectangle. If you don't know the special and exciting properties of these geometric figures, go online to the math primer. If you do know, then you'll be able to at least formulate the correct equation for line *EC*, but then you *still* have to crunch the numbers to solve it. Let's see what a solid effort on this question might look like.

First, you're best off redrawing the diagram on your scratch paper, because you wouldn't want to keep all the information you're going to add to it in your head. If *AB* and *BC* are equal, ∠*BAC* and ∠*BCA* must be equal because the **angles in a triangle opposite from equal sides are equal** (concept 1). The third angle labeled *x* equals 60°, so ∠*BAC* and ∠*BCA* together must total 120° because the **three angles of a triangle add up to 180°** (concept 2). We determined that ∠*BAC* and ∠*BCA* are equal, so they both must be 60°. Notice anything now? **A triangle with three equal angles is an equilateral triangle** (concept 3). Because **all three sides in an equilateral triangle are equal** (concept 4), *AB* = *BC* = *AC* = 4. Since *ACDE* is a rectangle, and **opposite sides of a rectangle are equal** (concept 5), *AC* = *ED* = 4. By now you're sketch should look like this:

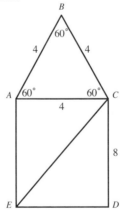

Now that we have two sides of right triangle ECD, we have everything we need to figure out the length of EC, thanks to the **Pythagorean theorem**: $x^2 + y^2 = z^2$ where x and y are the sides and z is the hypotenuse (concept 6). Substituting 4 and 8 as the sides and EC as the hypotenuse gives us:

$$(EC)^2 = 4^2 + 8^2 =$$

For convenience, we'll denote all of the ensuing **arithmetic**, including **simplifying the radical**, as concept 7:

$$\left(EC\right)^2 = 4^2 + 8^2$$
$$\left(EC\right)^2 = 16 + 64$$
$$\left(EC\right)^2 = 80$$
$$EC = \sqrt{80}$$
$$EC = \sqrt{16}\sqrt{5}$$
$$EC = 4\sqrt{5}$$

Voila!—**B** is correct. Check out the traps: 4, **A**, is a number calculated along the way; 8, **D**, is a number given in the problem; and 12, **E**, is what you get if you add the two known sides of triangle ECD together.

Notice that no fewer than *seven* math concepts made their way into this problem—none of them particularly earth-shattering or treacherous, mind you, but still adding up to a medium-level challenge with plenty of potential pitfalls.

Essential Concept #2:
Alternative Approaches for Special Cases

The standard "do question, look for answer" approach is all well and good in many cases, but some questions call out for alternative approaches. When the question contains variables in the answer choices, *making up numbers* and *substituting* them into the problem is often very effective. Conversely, when the answer choices contain actual numbers, you may benefit from simply plugging them back into the given situation to see which one works, instead of hacking through some difficult arithmetic or algebra. This is called *working backward*. Let's take a look at each of these approaches, one by one.

MAKING UP NUMBERS

Which of the following problems would you rather be faced with on test day?

- **Question 1:** If x apples cost y cents, how much will z apples cost in dollars?
- **Question 2:** If 5 apples cost 50 cents, how much will 10 apples cost in dollars?

If you're like most people, question 2 looks much easier, and you probably wouldn't have much trouble solving it: If you double the number of apples, you double the number of cents. One hundred cents equals one dollar. Done.

The difference between question 1 and question 2 is simple. We replaced the variables in question 1 with some made-up numbers, thus creating the easier question 2. So if you see x, y, m, n, or any other variables in both the question and the answer choices, consider avoiding complicated algebra by making up numbers and inserting them into the problem. You don't want to just make up any old numbers, however. You want numbers that will simplify the problem.

Use the following guidelines:

- **Pick easy numbers.** Although you could choose 582.97 as a value, you definitely wouldn't be making the problem any easier. Stick to relatively small, whole numbers whenever possible.

- **Avoid 0, 1, and any numbers used in the problem.** The numbers 0 and 1 have unique properties that may skew the results when used for this technique, so don't substitute either of those into the problem. Also, because the test makers sometimes use numbers from the question to construct distractors, you may get yourself into trouble by selecting those as well. If, for example, the problem contains the expression $3a + 5$, don't use 3 or 5. You shouldn't have any trouble avoiding the few numbers used in the question itself, just for good measure.

- **Choose different numbers for different variables.** For example, if the problem contains the variables m and n, you wouldn't want to choose 2 for both. Instead, you might choose 2 for m and 3 for n.

- **Pay attention to units.** If a problem involves a change in units (such as minutes to hours, pennies to dollars, feet to yards, and so on), choose a number that works well for both units. For example, 120 would be a good choice for a variable representing minutes because 120 minutes is easily converted into 2 hours.

- **Obey the rules of the problem.** Occasionally, the problem may include specific requirements for variables. For example, if the problem says that x must be negative, you can't make up a positive value for x.

- **Save dependent variables for last.** If the value of one variable is determined by the value of one or more other variables, make up numbers for those other variables first. That will automatically determine the value of the variable that depends on the value of the others. For example, if the problem states that $a = b + c$, a is dependent on b and c. Choose values for b and c first, and the value of a will then simply emerge as the sum of b and c.

Once you've selected your values, an actual number will emerge when you work the problem out with the numbers you've selected. All you need to do then is check which answer choice contains an expression that yields the same value when you make the same substitutions. This will make more sense in the context of an example, so let's check one out.

A gear makes r rotations in m minutes. If it rotates at a constant speed, how many rotations will the gear make in h hours?

(A) $\dfrac{60r}{m}$

(B) $\dfrac{60rh}{m}$

(C) $\dfrac{60rm}{h}$

(D) $\dfrac{rh}{m}$

(E) $\dfrac{mrh}{60}$

Sure, you could crunch through this algebraically, and if that floats your boat, great. However, if you're among those who get a headache from just looking at questions like this, making up numbers may be just the way to go. Here's how.

The variables in this problem are r, m, and h. We can make up whatever values we'd like for these, as long as the values we choose make it easy to work the problem. For r, the number of rotations, let's choose something small, like 3. For m, the number of minutes, we should choose a value that will make it easy to convert to hours: 120 works well because 120 minutes is the same as 2 hours. Finally, for h, we should choose something small again.

Remember that we need to choose a different value for each variable, so let's use 4. Now that we have our numbers, simply plug them into the situation:

> A gear makes **3** rotations in **120** minutes. If it rotates at a constant speed, how many rotations will the gear make in **4** hours?

Okay, much better—that's something we can sink our teeth into. 120 minutes is the same as 2 hours, during which time the gear rotates 3 times. If it rotates 3 times in 2 hours, how many times will it rotate in 4 hours? That's just twice as much time, so it will make twice as many rotations: $2 \times 3 = 6$, and so 6 is what we get when we substitute our values into the problem. Now we have to find the answer choice that's equal to 6 when the same values are substituted for its variables. Just work your way down the list, using 3 for r, 120 for m, and 4 for h:

A: $\dfrac{60r}{m} = \dfrac{(60)(3)}{120} = \dfrac{180}{20} = \dfrac{3}{2}$: That's not 6, the answer we seek, so move on.

B: $\dfrac{60rh}{m} = \dfrac{(60)(3)(4)}{120} = \dfrac{720}{120} = 6$: Yup—this is exactly what we're looking for,

so **B** is correct. If you're sure of your work, there's no need to even continue with the choices; you'd just pick **B** and move on to the next question. For practice, though, let's see how the other three pan out:

C: $\dfrac{60rm}{h} = \dfrac{(60)(3)(120)}{4} = 5,400$: Way too big.

D: $\dfrac{rh}{m} = \dfrac{(3)(4)}{120} = \dfrac{1}{10}$: Way too small.

E: $\dfrac{mrh}{60} = \dfrac{(120)(3)(4)}{60} = 24$: Four times bigger than what we're after.

Just what we thought: **B** is the only choice that matches the number we derived from our made-up numbers, so **B** gets the point.

.I'll get more practice with this strategy as we go forward. Let's now move on to our other specialty technique, an exercise in role reversal that we call . . .

WORKING BACKWARD

When the question includes an equation (or a word problem that can be translated into an equation), and the answer choices contain fairly simple numbers, then it may be possible to plug the choices back into the equation to see which one works. You can't work backward on Grid-Ins, though, because those questions don't have answer choices.

Working backward from the choices may help you avoid setting up or solving complicated equations and can save you time as well because of a neat wrinkle of this technique: The choices in math questions are usually written in either ascending or descending order, so you can start with the middle choice, **C**, and either get the answer immediately or at least eliminate three choices for the price of one. Here's how.

Let's say the answer choices are in ascending order. If you start by plugging in **C**, then even if that choice doesn't work, you can use the outcome to determine whether you need to plug in a smaller or larger number. If you need a smaller number, then **D** and **E** are out of the question, and you can go right to **A** or **B**. If, instead, you need a larger number, chop **A** and **B** and try **D** or **E**. Notice another nice feature: When you plug in for the second time, that choice will either work or leave only one choice standing. If you follow this alternative approach, you shouldn't ever have to check more than two choices. Because working backward requires you to work with the answer choices, you won't be able to use this strategy on grid-ins.

As always, math strategies make the most sense in the context of examples, so we'll demonstrate using the following question, which we discussed in the X-ray.

A classroom contains 31 chairs, each of which has either a cushion or a hard back. If the room has five more cushion chairs than hard-backed chairs, how many cushion chairs does it contain?

(A) 10
(B) 13
(C) 16
(D) 18
(E) 21

Now if you happen to be an algebra whiz, you'd go ahead and use the information to set up a pair of simultaneous equations to solve the problem. However, you may find it easier to work backward instead. The choices are in ascending order, so we'll start with the middle one and pretend it's correct. If it really *is* correct, then plugging it into the problem's scenario will cause all the numbers to work out, so let's see if it does.

The question is looking for the number of cushion chairs, which for the moment we're assuming to be 16. We can bounce that number off the information in the beginning of the second sentence (5 more cushion chairs than hard chairs) to determine that with 16 cushion chairs, there would have to be 11 hard chairs. Now all we have to do is check whether this scenario matches the information in the first sentence. Would that give us 31 chairs total? Nope: $16 + 11 = 27$, so the numbers don't jibe. That tells us three things: **C** isn't correct, **B** isn't correct, and **A** isn't correct. We can knock out **A** and **B** along with **C** because they're both *smaller* than **C**, and if the number in **C** isn't big enough to get us to our required 31 chairs, **A** and **B** ain't gonna cut it either.

Now let's try **D**—if it works, it's correct, and if it doesn't, we can select **E** without even trying it out: 18 cushion chairs means 18 – 5 = 13 hard chairs and 18 + 13 = 31 chairs total. That matches the information in the question, so **D** is correct. Note that you could have worked the numbers the other way: If there are 31 chairs total, and we assume there are 18 cushion chairs, then there would have to be 13 hard chairs. That matches the information in the second sentence that requires 5 more cushion chairs than hard ones. Either way you slice it, the number 18 fits the bill when plugged back into the situation, and we didn't have to bother with creating and solving simultaneous equations.

Standard vs. Alternative Approaches

We want to stress that neither an alternative approach nor the standard approach is necessarily better. There are faster and slower ways, depending on your strengths in math. Of course, it always benefits you to use the faster way if you can, but the most important thing is getting the question right.

Trying to solve problems using the standard approach is conceptually demanding but can take less time. Working backward or making up numbers makes questions easier to tackle but will likely take more time. Use your judgment as to when to work backward. If there are numbers in the answer choices, then consider it, but don't do it if the numbers are unwieldy, such as complex fractions. One of the skills that the best math test takers possess is the ability to determine the most effective way to work through the problems. We've shown you standard applications and a few powerful alternatives. In the next section, we'll review some Essential Strategies, as well as the general step method, that you can use on all SAT Math questions.

ESSENTIAL STRATEGIES

Here are the math strategies to keep in mind on test day:

- Draw Pictures
- Use Your Calculator Wisely
- Eyeball
- Use the SAT Math Step Method

Draw Pictures

Take advantage of the white space in your SAT test booklet. You can use this space to write formulas or draw graphs, triangles, or whatever else you want. This space can be particularly useful for drawing figures that are not provided with the question. If you have a hard time visualizing shapes in your head, draw them in the test booklet. If a question asks you about a polygon but doesn't provide a figure, you can draw one of your own if it will help you solve the problem.

Although writing out your answers or drawing figures can be extremely helpful, it can also be time consuming. No one will see your test booklet, so don't worry about trying to be neat or artistic. Do just as much writing or drawing as you need to do in order to get the question right—no more, no less.

Use Your Calculator Wisely

Just because you are permitted to use your calculator on the SAT doesn't mean that you should go calculator crazy. Every question on the SAT can be solved without using a calculator, so you never *need* to start pushing buttons. Calculators can certainly be helpful on some problems, but on others using a calculator might actually take more time than working the problems out by hand.

When you use your calculator on the test, it should be because you have thought about the question, have a good sense of how to proceed, and see how your calculator can help you. Keep the following "do's and don'ts" in mind:

- **Do** use a calculator for any brute-force tasks, such as dealing with decimals.
- **Don't** use your calculator if you have to deal with a long string of numbers. Instead, look for a way to cancel out some of the terms and simplify. A way will usually exist.
- **Don't** use your calculator on fraction problems or on algebra questions with variables.
- **Do** know how to use your calculator before the test. Be comfortable and familiar with it so you don't waste time fiddling with buttons during the test. This is particularly true of graphing calculators.

Above all else, remember: Your calculator is a tool. You wouldn't wildly swing a hammer around, but some students seem to think they can just whip out their calculator and it will magically solve their problems. Those students seldom do well on SAT Math.

Eyeball

Always remember to use your eyes. Seriously. Sometimes a quick look lets you eliminate a few choices.

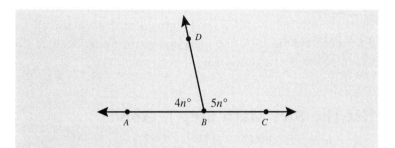

If $\overline{AC}$ is a line, which of the following is the measurement of $\angle DBC$?

(A)   20°
(B)   80°
(C)   100°
(D)   110°
(E)   160°

Just eyeball $\angle DBC$ and ask yourself, "Is this angle greater than or less than 90°?" Everyone has a good idea what a 90° angle looks like.

$\angle DBC$ is a little more than 90°. Not much, but a bit more. Scanning the answer choices, you can eliminate **A** and **E** quickly because both are way off base. **B**, 80°, is closer, but it's less than 90°, so it's unlikely to be the correct answer. That leaves us with **C** and **D**. There's no way to use your eyes to make a 10° call one way or the other, but for a 50/50 chance, you can guess, which is well ahead of the wrong-answer penalty. The answer, by the way, is **C**:

$$4n + 5n = 180$$
$$9n = 180$$
$$n = 20$$
$$\angle DBC = 5n$$
$$\angle DBC = 100$$

The test makers will always tell you if a figure is not drawn to scale. If you don't understand the math, then using your eyes on figures can often give you a good shot at a tough question.

Use the SAT Math Step Method

Here's the method to use on every math question you'll see on test day:

Step 1: Get the Specs.

Step 2: Plan the Attack.

Step 3: Mine the Math.

Step 4: Power Through.

Before we work out some sample problems, let's see how the steps work:

Step 1: Get the Specs. Step 1 puts you in the right frame of mind to successfully work through a math question. The main specifications that should interest you include the following:

- Is it a multiple-choice question or a grid-in?
- What general subject area—arithmetic, algebra, geometry, or data analysis—is being tested?

Step 2: Plan the Attack. In Step 2, you'll determine your approach—that is, whether you'll use the standard approach and then search the choices for the answer you get, or whether it's better to make up numbers or work backward. Use the information you discovered in Step 1 to help you decide how to proceed.

Step 3: Mine the Math. With a solid plan in mind, you'll then dig through your math knowledge to figure out what you need to use to solve the problem. If the question concerns a right triangle, for example, then the Pythagorean theorem and rules for the length of the sides of right triangles should pop into your head. If you were up against exponents, an arithmetic mean situation, or a quadratic equation, you'd pull concepts related to those topics from your reservoir of math knowledge. Don't think you have to gather every single concept you'll need at this stage; some necessary concepts will emerge as you proceed through the problem in Step 4. In Step 3, simply dig out the math you need to get started.

Step 4: Power Through. With the relevant math and a plan firmly in mind, you'll now be able to power through the question. "Power through," however, doesn't necessarily imply using brute force, for in many cases, clever or elegant solutions may be possible. How you do the work will depend on the method you choose in Step 2, and in many cases the standard approach works fine. But in other cases you may settle on one of the alternative approaches. Either way, Step 4 is the time to solve the problem.

Let's work through some examples of multiple choice and grid-ins.

> If the average (arithmetic mean) of 13, 6, 9, x, and y is 12, what is the
> average of $x + y$?
>
> (A)   6
> (B)   9
> (C)   12
> (D)   16
> (E)   32

Step 1: Get the Specs. Here we have a multiple-choice problem, which draws on our knowledge of algebra.

Step 2: Plan the Attack. We need to find the average of the five-item set and then the average of the missing two pieces. Let's use the standard application of math concepts.

Step 3: Mine the Math. Based on our Step 2 plan, we know we need the **mean/average equation**:

$$\text{mean} = \frac{\textbf{sum of all items}}{\textbf{number of all items}}$$

Step 4: Power Through. Now that we know what to do, it's time to do the math. The average of the five items is 12, $12 = \dfrac{\text{sum}}{5}$. So the sum is 60. If the sum is 60, and three of the items are 13, 6, and 9, then the sum of the last two must be $60 - (13 + 6 + 9)$, or 32.

We're not quite done yet. 32 looks pretty good, and it's one of the answer choices, but *it's not what the question asked for.* To find their average, divide 32 by 2 to get 16.

The correct answer is **D**, 16.

Here's another example:

> If $5x + 18 = 63$, what is the value of x?
>
> (A)   5
> (B)   9
> (C)   13
> (D)   17
> (E)   40

Step 1: Get the Specs. This multiple-choice question gives us an algebraic equation, then asks us to figure out the value of the variable x.

Step 2: Plan the Attack. There are two ways to find x. We could work through the equation, manipulating the numbers as necessary until we isolate x. Or we could work backward, plugging the values into the equation. That option sounds good.

Step 3: Mine the Math. We're working backward and plugging in the values, so there's no math to mine. We can head straight to Step 4.

Step 4: Power Through. Start with **C**: $5(13) + 18 = 65 + 18 = 83$. That's too high, so **C** is too big. **D** and **E** are even bigger, so they must also be wrong. That leaves **A** and **B**.

We have to try only one of them to get the answer. Let's say we start with **A**: $5(5) + 18 = 25 + 18 = 43$. That's too low, so **A** is too small. That leaves **B**, which is correct. And sure enough: $5(9) + 18 = 45 + 18 = 63$.

Now we'll use the math step method to work through some grid-ins.

What is 0.5 percent of 55?

Step 1: Get the Specs. Not much to it, is there? It's a grid-in, with straight arithmetic. Nothing too crazy.

Step 2: Plan the Attack. A straightforward approach is the way to go. We'll dig out the math concept we need and use it to do the math.

Step 3: Mine the Math. Adding the word percent to a number means taking that number two places to the left when converting it to a decimal. For example, 20 percent = 0.2. In this example, 0.5 percent = 0.005. The other thing you need to know is that the word *of* **means "multiplication"; whenever we take a certain percent of something, we multiply the figures**.

Step 4: Power Through. Let's do the math: $005 \times 55 = 0.275$, so you'd grid-in ".", "2," "7," and "5" on your answer sheet. Maybe you just multiplied it out by hand, or instead used approximations to get into the ballpark. Here's one way you can work through it without actually multiplying: 10 percent of 55 is 5.5, so to get 1 percent of 55, we just move the decimal place back one more place, giving us 0.55. Now, 0.5 percent is half of 1 percent, so we have to divide 0.55 by 2, which gives us 0.275.

Though the question is a straightforward test of your arithmetic knowledge, there are still a few concepts you need to know, some steps you need to perform, and some traps that could potentially trip you up.

Here's another grid-in:

> A clothes designer must choose 3 of 10 possible fabrics for a single outfit. What is the total number of different outfits that the designer can create given this requirement?

Step 1: Get the Specs. The lingo in this grid-in should alert you immediately to what you're up against—*choose 3 of 10 possible fabrics* indicates that this is either a **permutation** or **combination problem**. The question is, which type of data analysis is it? We'll settle that matter in Step 3 when we dig down into our stockpile of useful math information.

Step 2: Plan the Attack. Permutation and combination problems require little more than crunching through a formula, so our plan will be to take a standard approach, work through the formula, and solve. Of course, you have to *know* the formula to use, so the battle in this one is pretty much won or lost in Step 3.

Step 3: Mine the Math. The key to determining whether to use the combination or permutation formula is figuring out whether order is significant. In a race or ranking, clearly order matters. But in an *outfit*? Does anyone look at an outfit and say "Hey, that outfit has some wool, and after that it has some polyester"? No, of course not. If it has both, it has both—it doesn't contain one before the other. Order is significant in permutations but not in combinations, so we're in combination territory. The combination formula is:

$$_nC_r = \frac{n!}{(n-r)!r!}$$

where unordered subgroups of size r are selected from a set of size n. **A factorial (!) following a number represents the product of all the numbers up to and including that number.**

Step 4: Power Through. If you know what permutations and combinations are, how to determine which to use in which circumstances, and the formulas and how to solve them, then the rest is definitely doable. As we said above, the battle in this question takes place primarily in Step 3. If you know all the concepts discussed in the previous step, the rest is little more than number crunching. Here goes:

$$_{10}C_3 = \frac{10!}{(10-3)!3!}$$
$$= \frac{10!}{7!3!}$$
$$= \frac{10 \times 9 \times 8 \times 7!}{7!3!}$$
$$= \frac{10 \times 9 \times 8}{3 \times 2 \times 1} = \frac{720}{6} = 120$$

The answer is **120**, so you'd grid that in on your answer sheet. Let's try another problem.

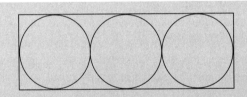

If the area of each of the three identical circles inscribed in the rectangle above is 25π, what is the perimeter of the rectangle?

This grid-in's a toughie. We'll cut it down to size using our step method:

Step 1: Get the Specs. A nifty little circle/rectangle picture comes along with this geometry question, so we may need to employ some creative visualization to see how a part of one shape tells us what we need to know about the other. This is definitely a multiple-concept question because we need to draw on our knowledge of multiple geometric shapes.

Step 2: Plan the Attack. There's no alternative approach to use here, so we'll just apply what we know about circles and rectangles to get the information we need to solve the problem.

Step 3: Mine the Math. Here are the geometry math concepts we'll need: **The area of a circle = πr²,** *where r is the radius.* **The diameter of a circle = twice its radius,** 2r. **The perimeter of a rectangle = the sum of its sides.**

Step 4: Power Through. Did you see the relationship between the three circles and the rectangle's perimeter? The width of the rectangle is equal to the diameter of each circle, whereas the length of the rectangle equals the diameter of the first circle + the diameter of the second circle + the diameter of the third circle. So if we find the diameter of the circles (all equal because the circles are identical), then we can find the rectangle's perimeter.

Start with what we know: The area of each circle is 25π. Plugging that into our area formula, we get:

$$\text{area} = \pi r^2$$
$$25\pi = \pi r^2$$
$$25 = r^2$$
$$r = 5$$

If the radius of each circle is 5, then the diameter of each side is 10. The width of the rectangle is therefore 10, and its length is $10 + 10 + 10 = 30$. The rectangle therefore has two sides of width 10 and two sides of length 30. The perimeter is therefore $10 + 10 + 30 + 30 = $ **80.** We'll grid it in and call it a day. Speaking of grid-ins, we want to go over a few special tips that will help you on test day.

SPECIAL ADVICE FOR GRID-INS

Keep these tips in mind when tackling grid-ins:

- **Write it out.** The computer that grades the SAT can't read anything but the ovals, so you don't have to write anything in the spaces at the top. However, filling in the spaces at the top might help you to avoid making careless mistakes. So just write it out.

- **There may be more than one correct answer to each problem.** You're probably accustomed to the "only one correct choice" mind-set brought on by excessive multiple-choice preparation. Grid-ins are different. Sometimes your answer will actually be a range of answers, such as "any number between 4 and 5." When that happens, pick one number that fits the criteria—i.e., 4.1, 4.2, or 4.6.

- **Answers can never be negative numbers.** All grid-ins must be positive (or zero, which is neither negative nor positive). If you come up with more than one answer, be sure to choose one that is a positive number. If you come up with a negative answer, you know you've made a mistake working out the problem.

- **Improper fractions must be simplified or converted to a decimal answer.** For example, $4\frac{1}{2}$ must be written as $\frac{9}{2}$ or 4.5. If you were to try to grid that answer in as $4\frac{1}{2}$, the computer that scans your answer sheet would read it as 41/2.

PRACTICE SET

Several multiple-choice questions and grid-ins follow. As always, remember the strategies and step method. Don't forget to read the explanations to every question.

1. Which of the following fractions is in its simplest reduced form?

    (A) $\dfrac{17}{136}$

    (B) $\dfrac{7}{126}$

    (C) $\dfrac{13}{69}$

    (D) $\dfrac{11}{121}$

    (E) $\dfrac{5}{160}$

2. In the arithmetic sequence $(5, 9, 13, 17, \ldots)$, where $n_1 = 5$, what is the value of n_8?

    (A) 29
    (B) 33
    (C) 37
    (D) 41
    (E) 45

Questions 3 and 4 refer to the following graph.

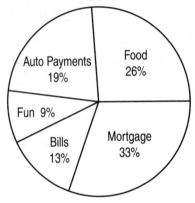

Monthly Household Income = $2, 400

The pie chart above represents the monthly distribution of family X's income.

3. According to the graph, how much is family X's mortgage in dollars?

    (A) 216
    (B) 312
    (C) 456
    (D) 624
    (E) 792

4. If family X completed all its car payments and transferred all the auto money into the "Fun" budget, then family X would most nearly spend the same amount on fun as they spend on

    (A) food
    (B) mortgage
    (C) bills
    (D) food and bills
    (E) food and mortgage

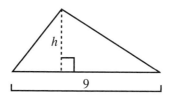

5. If the triangle above has an area of 27, then $h =$

$\frac{1}{2}9(x) = 27$

(A) 3
(B) 5
(C) 6
(D) 8
(E) 10

6. The circle above has been divided into three congruent segments. If the circumference of the circle is 12π, what is the area of one segment?

(A) 4π
(B) 6π
(C) 12π
(D) 24π
(E) 36π

7. A retail outlet is having a clearance sale on all the shoes in its inventory over a period of four days. On the first day it sells $\frac{1}{4}$ of its inventory, on the second day it sells $\frac{1}{2}$ of the remaining inventory, and on the third day it sells $\frac{1}{6}$ of the remainder. What fraction of the original inventory is left for the last day of the sale?

(A) $\frac{1}{12}$

(B) $\frac{1}{10}$

(C) $\frac{1}{8}$

(D) $\frac{5}{16}$

(E) $\frac{5}{8}$

8. Six years ago, June was twice the age of Sue and 8 years older than Bill. If Bill is now x years old, then in terms of x, what is Sue's current age?

(A) $x + 8$

(B) $\frac{x+8}{2}$

(C) $\frac{(x-6)+8}{2} + 6$

(D) $\frac{x+8}{2} + 6$

(E) $\frac{(x-6)+8}{2x}$

9. If $4^x = 64^{12}$, what is the value of $\left(\sqrt[3]{\sqrt{2}}\right)^x$?

(A) 2^{36}
(B) 2^{24}
(C) 2^{16}
(D) 2^{12}
(E) 2^6

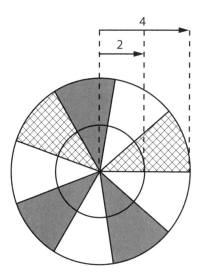

Note: All 9 arc sectors are of equal area.

10. If one dart is thrown at the figure above, what is the probability of it hitting the white regions of the inner circle?

(A) $\dfrac{1}{9}$

(B) $\dfrac{2}{9}$

(C) $\dfrac{1}{3}$

(D) $\dfrac{4}{9}$

(E) $\dfrac{5}{9}$

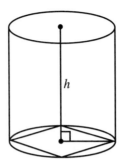

h

Note: Figure not drawn to scale.

11. A square is inscribed in the base of a right circular cylinder of height 3. If the area of the square is 4, then what is the volume of the cylinder?

(A) 6π
(B) $6\pi\sqrt{2}$
(C) 12π
(D) $12\pi\sqrt{2}$
(E) 36π

12. If $f(x) = x^2 - 2x$, what does $f(6)$ equal?

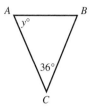

13. If $AC = BC$, then $y = ?$

14. There are 3, 600 pieces of candy divided into three different colors: red, blue, and green. There are more blue pieces than red and more green pieces than blue. If there are 1,000 red pieces, what is the LARGEST amount of blue pieces possible?

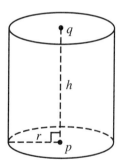

15. The volume of the right circular cylinder pictured above is 81π. If the height of the cylinder is three times the radius, what is the diameter of circle P?

Guided Explanations

1. C

Simple fractions are fractions that can't be reduced any more. Four of the answer choices can be reduced. Your goal is to find the one that can't.

Take a first pass through the answer choices and see whether there are any obvious choices for further reduction. **E** springs to mind because the 5 in the numerator could easily go into the 160 in the denominator. This fraction can actually be reduced, but why? It's enough to realize that it *can* be reduced. Once you determine that, cross it out and move on.

The remaining answer choices all contain prime numbers in their numerators. This is good news because it means you now only have to use your calculator and try to divide the lower number (denominator) by the upper number (numerator).

For **A**, you punch in 136 ÷ 17 = 8. Because this is a whole number, this fraction can be reduced. Cross out **A** and keep chugging. **B**: 126 ÷ 7 = 18. Nope. **C**: 69 ÷ 13 = 5.307 something. **C** can't be reduced. It's your answer.

2. B

You can tackle sequence questions by going all algebraic and setting up a nifty little formula to solve them. But this is not the smartest path on the SAT. The main reason it's a bad idea is that all the distractors are set up to trap students who do all the math. You play right into the SAT's hands by tackling a question in this manner. This doesn't mean you won't get it right. It just means you run a much greater risk of getting it wrong because the incorrect answer choices are all designed to catch people who make a mistake working the algebra.

So go low-tech instead. *Write stuff out.* You should write work down on every question, every time, and solve the questions on paper, not in your head. For this sequence question, take 15 seconds to write out:

n1	n2	n3	n4	n5	n6	n7	n8

Now place the numbers given to you in the stem underneath:

n1	n2	n3	n4	n5	n6	n7	n8
5	9	13	17				

As you can see, 4 is added to each number in the sequence. Finish up the list, and you have your answer. Furthermore, you know it's right, *and* you can come back and check your work very easily if you have the time at the end of the section. Those last two points are just as important as the first one.

n1	n2	n3	n4	n5	n6	n7	n8
5	9	13	17	21	25	29	33

B is 33.

3. E

Because pie charts often show percentages—like this one—they are often accompanied by a real number, such as "Monthly Household Income = $2,400." This allows the test makers to fashion questions like this one, where you have to find the right percentage, then convert this to a dollar amount.

The conversion is fairly straightforward. If the mortgage is 33% of the total monthly income, and this income is $2,400, then:

$$(33\%)(\$2,400) = (0.33)(\$2,400) = \$792$$

That's **E**.

4. A

Auto Payment and *Fun* are right next to each other—imagine erasing the line between the two. You would now have a new pie piece. To paraphrase the problem, your goal is to find an old pie piece that is the same size as this new "Auto Payments plus Fun" piece. The answer is literally right next to the new piece because *Food*, **A**, is roughly the same size as the new piece. This shouldn't be surprising because *Food* consists of 26% of the budget, and the new piece combines *Auto Payment* (19%) and *Fun* (9%). Together they combine to make 19% + 9% = 28%.

5. B

You have two figures, and you need to use the information about one figure (the square) to determine a number associated with the other figure (the circle). Because you have the area of the square, you can first determine the length of each side.

$$A = s^2$$
$$16 = s^2$$
$$\sqrt{16} = \sqrt{s^2}$$
$$4 = s$$

Each side of the square is length 4, and one side of the square is the diameter of the circle. This means the diameter of the circle is also 4. Because the

circumference of a circle is given by the formula $C = \pi d$, the circumference
is $C = \pi d = 4\pi$, **B**.

6. E

The problem mentions a rectangle, but don't be fooled. This is a triangle
problem dressed up as a rectangle problem. The diagonals are both hypote-
nuses of right triangles, so the **Pythagorean theorem** can be strutted out to
determine the length of each diagonal.

$$a^2 + b^2 = c^2$$
$$2^2 + 3^2 = AC^2$$
$$4 + 9 = AC^2$$
$$13 = AC^2$$
$$\sqrt{13} = AC$$

At this point, two things can happen. You can recall that **the diagonals
of a rectangle are always the same length**, or you can run through the
Pythagorean theorem again to figure the length of BD. Either way you get
$BD = \sqrt{13}$. Because the stem asks for the product of the two diagonals, you
now multiply: $(AC)(BC) = (\sqrt{13})(\sqrt{13}) = 13$ and end up with **E**.

Always be on the lookout for triangles!

7. D

The word problem is pushing for you to create some wickedly convoluted
algebraic formula involving all those fractions, but that's a sucker's game.
Instead, make up a number for the amount of shoes in the inventory before
it all goes down. We're going to use 80. In general, try to pick a fat, divisible
integer, and if you have to go to fractions, so be it. Some numbers will work

better than others, but if you do the math correctly, it won't matter what you started with. Now run through the computations:

80	number of shoes starting out
$80 - 20 = 60$	$\frac{1}{4}$ of 80 is 20, the amount sold on Day 1
$\frac{60}{2} = 30$	$\frac{1}{2}$ the remaining number is sold on Day 2
$30 - 5 = 25$	$\frac{1}{6}$ of 30 is 5, the amount sold on Day 3

So we started with 80 and ended up with 25. This fraction works out to be: $\frac{25}{80} = \frac{5}{16}$ **D**.

Just for kicks, try starting out with a different number. Either way, do the math right, and you'll end up at **D**.

8. C

Give June an age now, and you can figure everything out from there. Let's make her 20, so $J = 20$. Six years ago would make June age 14. If she was twice Sue's age at that time, $S = 7$. If June was 8 years older than Bill when she was 14, $B = 6$. We have:

$$J = 20$$
$$S = 7$$
$$B = 6$$

If x equals Bill's current age, then $x = 6 + 6 = 12$. Sue was 7 six years ago, so now she is 13.

Go through all the answer choices and replace each x with a 12. Then find the answer choice that works out to 13. **C**'s your answer.

9. D

To determine what $\sqrt[3]{2^x}$ is, you need to find a value for x. That's where the equation $4x = 64^{12}$ comes in.

Let's tackle the equation first. You could use your calculator and try to find the value of 64^{12}, but there's a better way to solve for x. You need to know how to manipulate exponents:

$$4^x = (64)^{12}$$
$$4^x = (4 \times 16)^{12}$$
$$4^x = (4 \times 4 \times 4)^{12}$$
$$4^x = (4^3)^{12}$$
$$4^x = 4^{36}$$

64 is the cube of 4. When you have an exponent taken to another exponent, you multiply the two numbers together, for example:

$$3 \times 12 = 36$$

This gives you a value for x of 36. When you take the cube root of a number with an exponent, you divide the exponent by 3. See what we mean about really knowing how to manipulate exponents?

$$(\sqrt[3]{2})^x = (\sqrt[3]{2})^{36} = 2^{\frac{36}{3}} = 2^{12}, \textbf{D}.$$

10. A

If you clutch to the OVER/UNDER method for **probability**, you have a chance on this one: **OVER = the number of favorable outcomes, and UNDER = total number of possible outcomes**. The goal is to think in terms of area. The UNDER portion is the area of the whole circular dartboard with a radius of 4.

$$\text{Area of circle} = \pi r^2 = \pi 4^2 = 16\pi$$

Doesn't look too promising, does it? Before you abandon all hope, let's look at the inner circle. The odds of hitting the inner circle alone would be computed the same way—by finding the area of the inner circle. But only 4 out of 9 inner circle pie sectors are white, so this number for inner circle area would then have to be multiplied by $\frac{4}{9}$. As ugly as it seems, this is the way to find the OVER value:

$$(\text{area of inner circle})\left(\frac{4}{9}\right) = \text{OVER value}$$

$$(\pi r^2)\left(\frac{4}{9}\right) = \left(\pi 2^2\right)\left(\frac{4}{9}\right) = \frac{16\pi}{9}$$

Never let it be said that the SAT doesn't award hard work. When we place the OVER value on top of the UNDER value, we get:

$$\frac{\text{OVER}}{\text{UNDER}} = \frac{\dfrac{16\pi}{9}}{16\pi} = \left(\frac{16\pi}{9}\right)\left(\frac{1}{16\pi}\right) = \frac{1}{9}$$

When you're dividing with fractions, you have to flip the value in the denominator over and then multiply. This makes 16π become $\frac{1}{16\pi}$, and then the 16πs cancel each other out. The answer is **A**.

11. A

The problem mentions cylinders and squares, but once again it's the unsung triangle that really brings home the bacon. The volume formula for the cylinder—one of the useful formulas provided to you at the beginning of the section—is $V = \pi r^2 h$. The height is given to you outright, and by now you are enough of a sleuth to realize that you have to take what's given (the area of the inscribed square) and manipulate this information to get the radius because that is what is needed for the volume formula.

Your journey is aided by the triangle within the inscribed square. Viewing the cylinder from above, it would look like this:

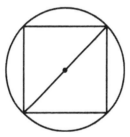

If the area is 4, then the side of the square is 2. Remember that two sides of a square and a diagonal form a 45-45-90 right triangle, which means that the hypotenuse will be the length of a side times $\sqrt{2}$. This makes the diagonal here equal to $2\sqrt{2}$. This diagonal is also a diameter. Because you only need a radius for the volume formula, you must cut it in two to get the radius value of $\sqrt{2}$. Place $\sqrt{2}$ into the volume formula and you get:

$$V = \pi r^2 h$$
$$V = \pi(\sqrt{2})^2 3$$
$$V = \pi(2)3$$
$$V = 6\pi$$

It's **A**.

12. 24

Follow the function:

$$f(x) = x^2 - 2x$$
$$f(6) = (6)^2 - 2(6)$$
$$f(6) = 36 - 12$$
$$f(6) = \mathbf{24}$$

13. 72

If $AC = BC$, then triangle ABC is an isosceles triangle. The angles opposite the equal sides are also equal, so $\angle ABC = \angle BAC$. $\angle BAC$ is just another name for angle y. Because the **sum of the interior angles of a triangle is 180**, set up the equation like this:

$$
\begin{aligned}
y + \angle ABC + 36 &= 180 \\
y + y + 36 &= 180 \\
2y &= 144 \\
y &= 72
\end{aligned}
$$

14. 1299

Let's take the question and convert it into Mathspeak. If there are more blue pieces than red ones, then B > R. If there are more green pieces than blue, G > B. We can combine these two terms and write:

$$G > B > R$$

Now we add 1,000 red pieces to the mix:

$$G > B > 1{,}000$$

If there are 3,600 pieces total, the amount of blue and green pieces must be 3,600 – 1,000 = 2,600. Half of this number is 1,300. If green has 1,301 pieces, and blue has 1,299 pieces, you have:

$$G > B > R$$
$$1{,}301 > 1{,}299 > 1{,}000$$

If you add more to the blue pieces, the green pieces would no longer outnumber them. So **1,299** is the greatest number of blue pieces you can have. Note, however, that you don't include commas in answers to grid-in questions.

15. 6

You're given the volume of the cylinder, and because that's the only number you have to work with, it's the best place to start. **The formula for the volume of a right circular cylinder is**

$$V = \pi r^2 h$$
$$81\pi = \pi r^2 h$$
$$81 = r^2 h$$

This might seem like the end of the road, but the question gives you one more fact: The height of the cylinder is three times the radius. A light might flash in your head at this point, but if not, just create an equation that shows this relationship:

$$h = 3r$$

Now place this into the formula above:

$$81 = r^2h$$
$$81 = r^2(3r)$$
$$81 = 3r^3$$
$$27 = r^3$$
$$3 = r$$

At this point, you might breathe a sigh of relief and then glibly place the number 3 in the grid. Don't! The question asks for the *diameter*, so the correct answer is twice the radius, **6**.

Top 15 SAT Test-Day Tips

HERE ARE OUR 15 TIPS FOR DOING YOUR BEST ON TEST DAY:

'Twas the Night Before the SAT . . .

#15: Get it together. Pack up the day before so that you don't have to go scrambling around in the morning. If you're bringing a calculator to use on the Math Test, make sure it has batteries. Get your admission ticket, ID, water, and nonsugar energy snack (for the break) all ready to go.

#14: Wind down. Runners don't run a full marathon the day *before*; they rest up for the big day. Avoid cramming the day before the test. Read a book, watch a movie, hang out with friends, whatever relaxes you—but make it an early night. And speaking of which . . .

#13: Get enough sleep. Don't get into bed at 7:00 just to stare at the ceiling, but do get to bed early enough to ensure you have enough sleep to be alert and energetic for test day.

#12: Set two alarms. You don't want to miss the test because your alarm was set for PM instead of AM—stranger things have happened. Also, one of your alarms should be battery-operated, just in case something crazy like a power outage occurs during the night. Unlikely, sure, but peace of mind will help you sleep better.

Rise and Shine . . .

#11: Eat normally. Sure, test day is special, but that doesn't mean you need to treat yourself to a special breakfast. Nerves can turn a huge bacon, egg, and cheese omelet against you—especially if you don't usually eat that kind of thing. Eat what you normally eat for breakfast—not too much, not too little. Bring a nonsugar snack for the break. It's a long day, and you'll need the energy.

#10: Dress for success. One word: *layers*. If it's hot, take some off. If it's cold, leave them on. Comfort is key.

#9: Jump-start your brain. To employ the marathon analogy again (see #14), runners stretch before the big event to warm up. Likewise, it helps to do a bit of reading before the test to get your mind warmed up and stretch those brain cells into shape. We're not talking Plato or Shakespeare here. Articles from a well-written newspaper, magazine, or journal containing the same kind of writing you'll see on the test will do.

Put on Your Game Face . . .

#8: Arrive early. Save fashionable lateness for your social life. Rushing around like a crazy person isn't the best way to start test day. If the testing center is in unfamiliar territory, you may even wish to scout it out ahead of time just to be sure you know your way. One less thing to worry about couldn't hurt.

#7: Don't sweat the small stuff. Okay, so what if it's 9 billion degrees in the testing room and that obnoxious kid from chem class is right next to you? If something potentially correctable is bothering you, by all means talk to a proctor, but if there's nothing you can do about it, *let it go*. Don't allow small annoyances to distract you from your mission.

#6: Gear up for a long haul. Some people arrive at the test center all revved up, bouncing off the walls—*the big day is finally here*! Slow down; you don't want to overheat and peak too soon. You'll get to the test site, endure the usual standardized testing bureaucratic technicalities, and probably fill out a bunch of paperwork. "Go time" isn't until the proctor tells you to open the test booklet. Which brings us to our tips for the final and most important phase of the testing experience . . .

Go Time . . .

#5: Prepare for the worst. This is by no means to say you should go in with a negative attitude, but you need to be ready to start the test by writing an essay on a topic of absolutely no interest to you, followed by your least favorite multiple-choice section. If something like that happens, you'll be prepared; if it doesn't, you'll be relieved. Win-win.

#4: Keep your focus. Maybe the girl to the right of you will appear to breeze through the first section in five minutes, while the guy to the left of you seems unaware that a test is even taking place. If you have a large enough group, chances are someone may even freak out and leave the room in tears. Assuming that this person isn't you, don't let it bother you. Stay focused on your objective and let the others take care of themselves.

#3: Choose your battles. No one question can hurt you significantly unless you spend all day on it. Keep moving through each section. If a question isn't working for you, guess and move on.

#2: Stick it out. There may come a time in the last section when you'll do anything to end your agony five minutes early. Hang in there and keep applying what you've learned. True champs finish strong.

And the #1 Test-Day Tip . . . Relax. Nerves are normal, but how you deal with them is up to you. Channel your adrenaline positively to give you the energy you need to maintain your focus all the way through. Also remember that while the test is surely important, *it's not the most important thing in the world*. Put the event into perspective. Then do the best you can, which is the most you can ask of yourself.

FINAL THOUGHT

Sure, maybe you could have started prepping sooner, but it's too late for that now. Banish the "coulda, woulda, shoulda" thoughts from your head and focus on the task at hand: doing your best on test day.

We at SparkNotes wish you the best of luck!

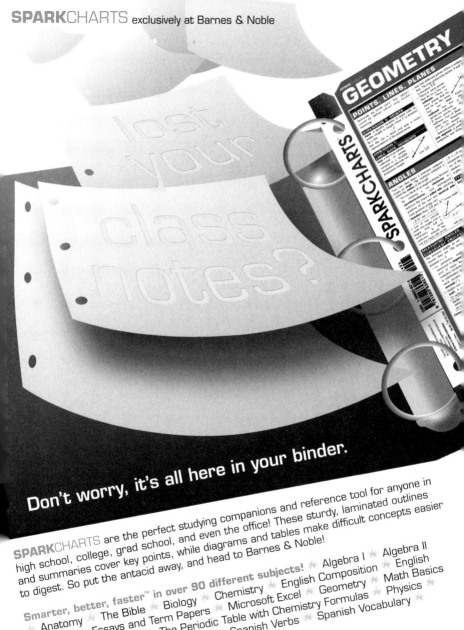